Praise

'There were so many things to consider when we were thinking about changing over from a gas boiler to a heat pump. We knew the most important thing was to have it installed properly. I desperately wished for a resource like this book to help us cut through the technical jargon and clarify the project's objectives. I would have particularly valued the section on the types of heat pump installers and how to choose between them. We lucked out and found an excellent local company that actually worked with us instead of just selling us a standard deal, but that was down to pure chance, not thoughtful planning!'

— **Christine Rigden**, Bedworth Church Eco-champion

'Warm Wisdom is a great starting point for any homeowner like me who is interested in getting a heat pump. Louise's book is full of practical advice, tips and things to watch out for from someone in the know. Reading this is like having your own friendly insider coach to talk you through everything you need to know in nontechnical language. I found the worked example of how to find a local installer particularly useful.'

— **Dr Amanda Salter**, Co-Founder, Astra

Warm Wisdom

A Stress-Free Guide to Finding and Fitting the Right Heat Pump for Your Home

Louise Howlett

Rethink

First published in Great Britain in 2026
by Rethink Press (www.rethinkpress.com)

Contents

Introduction

About two years ago I became frustrated by all of the conflicting messages in the press and online about heat pumps. As the owner of a small business that has specialised for seventeen years in heat pump installation, and as a homeowner who has lived with the technology for the same length of time, I have warm wisdom to share on the subject. In that sense I'm a heating expert, though I'm not a mechanical engineer or an installation technician. I am passionate about this industry and have perspective on where we are on the road to heat pumps becoming mainstream.

There are few women with this lived experience of the industry and the technology. Traditionally, women have been associated with prioritising a cosy home and turning the thermostat up. I fit that stereotype only in that I hate to be cold. It's not a problem I routinely face, though – I leave a cosy house and go to a warm commercial unit to work, both of which are heated by heat pumps.

Heat pumps: The decarbonisation imperative

Why are heat pumps so important? This is the first technology in human history that creates heat without combustion (or without *burning stuff*, as I like to phrase it). It is the need to burn fuels that leads to carbon emissions that, as a global community, we are desperately trying to reduce. Each person or household needs to go on their own journey with their transition from reliance on fossil fuels to lower-carbon alternatives. In *Warm Wisdom* I will support you with the heating aspect of that transition.

The origins of heat pump technology can be traced back almost two hundred years to the invention of modern refrigeration. The ability to harness and move heat – what both refrigerators and heat pumps do – is tied to the laws of physics. I mention the longevity to highlight that it is a mature technology and that it is available to us now, with no new inventions required. Heat pumps make lower carbon emissions possible and easily achievable.

Homeowner, industry insider and interpreter

When looking to replace their oil or gas boiler, most people are confused by a sea of conflicting information. In this book I'll show you that it isn't necessary to become a heating nerd to find the ideal solution. There are many new and exciting initiatives that make heat pumps more affordable to a wider spectrum of homeowners than ever before.

I contribute as spokesperson for the plumbing and heating industry through the Heating Trades Network, and I'm involved in a wider community of built environment professionals through Her Retrofit Space. Over the last couple of years I have engaged with my industry peers, working to implement a new apprenticeship to train heat pump engineers. My efforts have paid off: from September 2025, heat pump engineers are being trained in Norfolk on the Low-Carbon Heating Technician Apprenticeship.

In November 2024 my work was recognised at the H&V News Awards – the plumbing and heating equivalent of the Oscars. I received the Outstanding Achievement of the Year Award, with particular acknowledgement of my passion for growing the skills of the next generation of engineers and installers. I was attending the dinner as a judge and was genuinely surprised to hear I'd won the award, my first thought being, *I haven't finished my book yet!*

With my experience as a homeowner and as an industry insider, I can interpret what is going on in the industry and guide you through the decision-making process.

The good news is that there are artisan heating firms dotted all over the UK. Together with my husband Richard Brown MCIPHE, I have built one over the past twenty-three years. Admittedly, artisan might seem an unlikely term in the context of heating installation, with heating considered to be technical rather than creative or crafted. We regularly hear feedback from customers, though, saying it's a shame all of the immaculate copper pipework has to be covered by lagging!

I secretly feel (well not so secret anymore) there is a gender divide – the men love to show off their plant room and the women like to boast of their cosier home.

Being of service to our industry and its customers

There is so much innovation, collaboration and enthusiasm in the grassroots of this industry, countless skilled and talented heating professionals working incredibly hard to make the transition to lower temperature heating successful. There are some parallels between the growth of our industry and the emergence of motor vehicles almost 150 years ago. It wasn't until the 1960s that almost all families owned a car, and as we end our reliance on fossil fuels, heat pumps are on the same journey to normalisation.

If you are interested in future-proofing your home and heating, and if you want to contribute to the UK's net zero goals, this book is for you.

It is also perfect for you if you are looking to install microgeneration technologies such as solar photovoltaics (PV) that produce electricity, adding battery storage in combination with a heat pump system.

Warm Wisdom will:

- Reduce your confusion and associated stress about how to switch to a heat pump
- Help you to decide when will be the best time to find a heat pump installer, to suit your circumstances
- Give you confidence on the key questions to ask heat pump installers and understand what's involved in the installation process
- Clarify what you are trying to achieve by upgrading your home with renewable technologies, including the benefits for you and the planet
- Provide a single, coherent voice, allowing you to make sense of the technical squabbling that is so prevalent on social media forums

In the following chapters I have zoomed out before zooming right in, providing historical information about the technology before moving on to the context, with information on the current UK industry. After that I encourage you to look at your own house or project – your starting point – and share some nitty-gritty practical details of how to find an installer and what the process should look like. This is real insider warm wisdom that is hard to find anywhere else. I have included case studies to give you real-life examples of acquiring and living with heat pumps. At the end of the book you will find sections on industry deep dives and resources, together with a glossary, to give you further insight into and understanding of heat pumps. I want you to feel fully prepared and ready to succeed in your aim to get a terrific heat pump system. I want you to be able to join the club of low-carbon cosiness.

PART ONE

WHAT HEAT PUMPS ARE AND HOW YOU CAN PREPARE FOR THE SWITCH

ONE
History And Context

Before we move on to the practicalities of harnessing the wonders of heat pumps, I want to give some historical context. This chapter will give you a brief overview of the history of heat pumps, while uncovering the many advantages of this type of heating as well as some of the drawbacks of specific systems. If you have no interest in this background information, you can of course skip to Chapter Two. Keep this chapter in mind, though, in case you want to return to it to gain an understanding of the pros and cons of the different types of heat pumps.

A short history of heat pumps

The origin of heat pump technology can be traced back to scientists and innovators in the nineteenth century. Lord Kelvin is credited with sharing a vision of heat pumps in 1852. He predicted that 'a reverse heat engine' might be used for heating as well as cooling.[1] From the second half of the nineteenth century and throughout the twentieth century, the technologies that make heat pumps work were continually being refined and improved.

Heat pumps do not create heat; they *move* heat. To do this they rely on the refrigeration cycle, which involves four processes:

1. Evaporation
2. Compression
3. Condensation
4. Expansion

Heat pumps to the rescue

Switzerland suffered from fuel supply shortages during and after the First World War. Adversity often encourages creativity, and serious discussions began as early as 1918 on the practicalities of heating using heat pumps to make use of natural resources such as hydroelectric power.

These debates within the scientific and engineering community in Switzerland led to a 100-kW water source heat pump being designed and installed in Zurich City Hall in 1938. This installation remained in use until 2001.[2]

The first domestic heat pump

The earliest British heat pump that used water as the heat source was installed by pioneering Scottish engineer Graeme Haldane to heat his house on the Foswell Estate, Perthshire, in 1927.[3]

The UK's first commercial heat pump

In 1945 John Sumner installed a heat pump using the river as its heat source. The timing was not accidental, being tied to fuel shortages at the end of the Second World War.

Sumner's system was technically a great success, keeping the Norwich Corporation Electricity Department building in Norwich city centre warm. Sumner calculated that his Norwich heat pump saved the use of 1,180 tonnes over a 20-year lifespan.[4] This equates to a total reduction in CO2 emissions by 2,950 tonnes. The sad part of the story is that, once the postwar fuel shortages were a distant memory, the Electricity Board were no longer in favour of a machine that used only a third of the electricity of that used by normal resistance heating. Sumner reported: 'Despite a relatively long period of satisfactory running, the board dismantled and destroyed the plant.'

Sumner wrote a book, *Domestic Heat Pumps,* published in 1975, in which he continued to advocate the development and deployment of heat pumps at scale.[5] He recognised, however, that this would incur a loss of revenue for the Electricity Board. He touched on several issues that are eerily topical fifty years on, mentioning the need to ease peak demand on electricity. He also recognised the potential for homeowners to switch from heating oil to electricity via a heat pump, and he predicted a reduction in the use of coal, which in our current vocabulary equates to decarbonisation.

In the foreword of *Domestic Heat Pumps,* SD Barnes acknowledged that Sumner provided a strong warning of diminishing energy supplies. He said that this warning largely fell on deaf ears, and 'In particular, the energy industry was decidedly unhelpful; for profits lay in persuading the consumer to waste rather than conserve.' Barnes went on to say that the heat pump was considered a 'bogus invention' because it claimed to create energy from nothing.

Sumner doesn't talk about global warming, climate change or carbon emissions in his book. He debates when electricity will be produced by nuclear power stations and whether problems will be encountered from this. His main focus is on the fact that heat pump technology can reduce the use of fossil fuels thanks to its ability to produce over three kW of heat from one kW of electricity to run the system.[6]

These stories from the twentieth century highlight that heat pumps have been seen as a great solution in times of fuel crisis, and yet they have been marginalised by the big business interest behind the fossil fuel industry. Now in the twenty-first century our emphasis is shifting towards decarbonisation in an attempt to reverse the damage caused by global warming. Perhaps this time the outcome will be different.

An introduction to different types of heat pumps

Heat pump technology is versatile and can extract heat from many sources. This book focuses mainly on the air source heat pump because it is the most common and likely heat pump you will install in your home. I'll start, though, with an overview of all the different types:

1. Air source heat pump (ASHP)
2. Ground source heat pump (GSHP)
3. Water source heat pump (WSHP)
4. Exhaust air heat pump (EAHP)
5. Air-to-air heat pump (AAHP)

1. Air source heat pump (ASHP)

I will provide technical information about ASHP systems throughout this book. Here are a few facts to start us off:

- ASHPs are the heat pumps most used in domestic single dwellings.
- With an ASHP you have a box outside. It needs clear space around it for air to flow in and out. It benefits from being on a sunnier side of your property as the air being drawn in will be warmer. ASHPs also work well in shadier locations, but you should try to avoid a narrow corridor position as this can lead to discharged cold air being drawn back into the unit.
- An ASHP harnesses warmth from the air. The air is warmed by the sun even on a cold, cloudy day.
- An ASHP is a different way to heat your home because it's not burning fuel, which is what gas and oil boilers do.
- An ASHP requires a refrigerant to compress the heat.
- An ASHP is connected to a *wet system* (which is what we are used to in the UK), that is using *emitters* such as radiators, towel rails and underfloor heating (UFH), or a combination of both.

2. Ground source heat pump (GSHP)

GSHPs are the second most common type of heat pump in use in the UK. Here are the most important facts:

- GSHPs are generally suited to large properties, new-builds, conservation areas and multiple-occupancy buildings.
- GSHPs use heat stored in the ground as a heat source, from a depth of around 1.2 metres, where the heat remains at around 10C all year round. You don't need a unit outside. Instead, there is a small chamber lid that looks like a plastic manhole cover. Alternatively, boreholes can be drilled to a depth of 100 metres or more.
- GSHPs have an important role to play in decarbonisation, with brilliant commercial applications possible. Efficiencies of scale can be achieved by boreholing a street at a time, which is an efficient way to work as housing estates are built. Unfortunately, effective use of the best technologies is unlikely while the building industry in the UK is struggling to build houses profitably.[7] Heat pumps installed in the new-build sector are sometimes the cheapest available ASHP units. Other more enlightened housebuilders are installing shared ground loops, allowing for passive cooling as well as ground source heating.

- If you live in a conservation area or own a listed property, there can sometimes be challenges to gain planning approval for an ASHP. It is worth considering a GSHP, because although it is significantly more expensive to install, it is an even more energy-efficient alternative.
- An exciting alternative in the future would be boreholes as an infrastructure that could be paid for like a utility. Each house would have their own indoor unit.
- Another option is district heating for large buildings with a huge plant room fed from boreholes, which then allows heat distribution from a central point.
- Innovative solutions are possible, such as installing photovoltaic-thermal (PV-T) panels that can recharge boreholes with warm water, heated by the sun during the summer. This allows even higher efficiency during the heating season.

There are a few drawbacks to GSHPs:

- You are less likely to install a GSHP to heat your home due to the capital outlay needed for ground loops or boreholes. For ground loops there will be an additional cost of at least £5,000, and for boreholes an additional cost of £20,000 or more can be expected. Please note that costs of boreholes and ground collectors will alter over time.

- You need to consider the space required and disruption caused by digging in ground loops or having a drilling rig on your property.
- ASHPs are now able to deliver higher outputs – a better seasonal coefficient of performance (SCOP) – which reduces the running cost advantage that GSHPs used to have.

3. Water source heat pump (WSHP)

Water source heat pumps are like GSHPs, using coils of pipe to extract heat from the ambient water temperature in a lake or river. Many stately homes run WSHPs using their lake as the heat source. One of the key factors for a WSHP is having access to a year-round reliable water source. A small stream that dries up or a well where the water level drops is not suitable. The size of the body of water required is quite large – an average-sized garden pond is not sufficient.

4. Exhaust air heat pump (EAHP)

This is a lesser-known type of heat pump suitable for small properties with low heat losses such as apartments when they are being built, and EAHPs can be retrofitted in bungalows. EAHPs are particularly suited for installation into new-build apartments.

The unit looks like a fridge freezer and contains a hot water cylinder and controls; it is typically located inside the home, with no box outside. The unit includes ventilation, which is similar to mechanical ventilation with heat recovery (MVHR). Ducting needs to be installed, so it is not straightforward to retrofit in multiple storey properties. EAHPs can run radiators and UFH or be connected to a district heating system, ie providing heat to multiple properties.

5. Air-to-air heat pump (AAHP)

We all know what an air-to-air heat pump is; we just don't call it that. In the UK we call it air conditioning (or air con). You may not have considered that air conditioning units can produce heat, even if you have experienced this form of heating and cooling in modern hotels and other large commercial buildings. Many of these buildings don't have openable windows, which means we are completely reliant on the atmosphere and temperature created by AAHP units.

The unit outside looks similar to an ASHP unit, and it is connected to an internal wall-mounted unit that blows out cold or warm air.

There are considerable debates on whether air con is superior to an ASHP; here are some of the arguments:

Pros

- There is no need for a wet system, radiators or UFH.
- Air con is less expensive to install than a wet central heating system.
- It is possible to fit air con to provide cooling to a few areas of your house, and the equipment can be added completely separately from your central heating system.
- You can use the cooling function in the summer when solar PV production is at its peak; pairing these technologies can reduce running costs.
- AAHPs will soon attract a £2,500 BUS grant for whole house systems later in 2026.

Cons

- Air-to-air systems have not traditionally produced hot water. Whole-house solutions including hot water are just coming onto the market.
- It is expensive to run as 'central heating' (more expensive than an ASHP).
- Air con contains more refrigerant than an ASHP as it is needed throughout the system rather than just sealed into the outdoor unit.

Personally, I am not keen on AAHPs, except on hot days, because I don't like the heat produced by air con systems. Living with an AAHP system is very different to an ASHP; the units blow out warm air, creating a dry environment. They also switch on and off, creating a hot and cold effect, which is the opposite of a weather-compensated air source heat pump system.

Contemporary context

We saw in the first section of this chapter where heat pump technology has come from and in the second section what types of heat pump there are to choose from. Now let's consider the current state of the heat pump market in England and the key factors that have shaped it in recent years.

If you feel apprehensive and unsure about embarking on a journey to switch to a heat pump, you're not alone. I know this industry well, having been immersed in it for two decades, and yet I find conflicting messaging online, in the press and on social media really confusing.[8] I want to provide context to the messaging, empowering you to make an informed decision about the heating journey ahead of you.

Present demand for heat pumps

At the time of writing, the people who are most likely to invest in heat pump technology in the UK include:

- Homeowners who want to reduce their carbon footprint in the hope of slowing or reversing global warming
- Those who have the money available to pay for the installation costs – over and above the Boiler Upgrade Scheme (BUS) grant
- Large numbers of people who are investing now to save money on running costs during retirement, likely also adopting solar PV and battery storage
- Homeowners undertaking a renovation project or extension, where they are starting from scratch, needing a completely new system
- Self-builders, where installing this technology is obvious and often required by planning rules
- Wealthy owners of rural estate properties who are increasingly recognising the benefits of twenty-first-century technology in their properties[9]

Halcyon days

As I reflect now, comparing the heat pump landscape in 2026 with 'the good old days', I didn't appreciate the stability of the market between 2009 and 2019, when we had the Renewable Heat Incentive (RHI) to support sales. This scheme paid homeowners back over seven years, the amount of payments varying depending on the size of the ground or air source heat pump system. The level of payments was calculated to pay recipients the difference between a fossil fuel system and a renewable system. The RHI was criticised for paying out thousands of pounds to wealthy rural homeowners – often farmers upgrading their farmhouses or millionaires building dream homes.[10] RHI was guilty as charged in that respect; however, if the aim was to reduce carbon, it delivered perfectly, really encouraging homeowners to decarbonise.

This was the market where we at R A Brown Heating Services began our focus on heat pumps, at the time that the Microgeneration Certification Scheme (MCS) was born and the RHI incentive scheme began. MCS, a body for installers to register with, was created to provide a standard for the industry. Regulation is always required when the government is providing incentives or grants. For that decade we grew our business slowly and sustainably, completing some satisfying ground source as well as air source projects.

There were major drawbacks to the RHI, in that it wasn't scalable and the homeowner needed to have access to upfront capital.[11] Successive governments have been under pressure to stimulate heat pump adoption to the mass market of average income homeowners.

Winds of change

It was inevitable that someone in the corridors of power would play the joker card: *We should be tackling fuel poverty*, and this led to the launch of the Boiler Upgrade Scheme (BUS) grant in 2022, which threw the heat pump market completely off balance. The intended accessibility proved to be purely theoretical. Set in a global context of sharply rising equipment costs following the Covid pandemic, high interest rates and a cost-of-living crisis, ordinary homeowners were not feeling financially empowered to buy an expensive, new-fangled heating system.[12]

Meanwhile, the gas industry has been playing a smoke-and-mirrors game with hydrogen. Millions have been spent on researching the viability of mixing hydrogen into the mains gas grid. Theoretically, hydrogen is greener and would reduce carbon emissions while ensuring the survival of the gas industry for many decades into the future. However, hydrogen cannot straightforwardly replace natural gas or be blended with it – there are cost implications both for manufacturing and for the grid. There are also safety concerns, as hydrogen is much more explosive than natural gas. Hydrogen potentially has a role as a fuel for large industry that can't easily be moved to low carbon, but for domestic households we already have a great way to decarbonise – heat pumps.[13]

A key component in this David and Goliath battle – with heat pumps on one side and the fossil fuel industry on the other – is that the clear messaging needed from the government has been lacking.

Surveying the battlefield

Over the last few years it's been tough to be a specialist heat pump installer. At R A Brown Heating Services we know our services align with our values and that heat pump technology offers a future where burning fuel to keep warm is no longer necessary. However, the BUS grant, initially set at a paltry £5,000, immediately underperformed. In autumn 2023 it was increased to £7,500, which stimulated the utility companies to enter the market. They attempted to install heat pump systems for £8,000 in homes with around 150 square metres of floor area.

The country seemed to be holding its breath until after the general election in 2024. Other established SMEs around us were going under, but R A Brown Heating Services was solid enough to survive, retaining our technicians and apprentices.

In a global context, where there are more pressing issues than what heating fuel we're using, inspiring people to make the effort to replace their old boiler with a heat pump still feels like a battle. We need electricity prices to come down – even if only for heat pump adopters – and to build confidence.

We need greater understanding of and education about the journey to achieving reduced carbon output and lower long-term energy costs. This book can't create affordable finance or lower electricity prices, but it can build understanding and confidence.

Warm wisdom – key points

- **Context.** The history of heat pumps is a fascinating story of innovation. Historically, heat pumps have been hailed as a solution during fuel crises but have been marginalised by the fossil fuel industry. Now, with the critical focus on decarbonisation, we have a chance to reverse the past and finally embrace heat pumps as a key part of our energy future.

- **Types of heat pumps.** There are five different types, to suit any type of domestic or commercial application:

  - ASHPs – common for domestic single dwellings

  - GSHPs – for large properties, new-builds, conservation areas and multiple-occupancy buildings

  - WSHPs – usually requiring a large body of water such as a lake or river

  - EAHPs – ideal for apartments when they are being built, can be retrofitted in bungalows

- AAHPs (air con) – well established in hotels and large commercial buildings; not as suitable for central heating in a home

- **Developments.** The recent history of heat pumps in the UK has been as turbulent as its beginnings in the twentieth century. The RHI scheme encouraged homeowners to decarbonise, paying people back the difference between a fossil fuel system and a renewable system, but it was not scalable. The market was thrown off balance in 2022 by the new Boiler Upgrade Scheme (BUS) grant, which was set at £5,000. The current BUS grant (now £7,500) has stimulated the market, but high upfront costs remain a barrier for many.

TWO

Considerations And Perspectives

The fact that you're reading *Warm Wisdom* shows that you are already considering the need to invest in a heat pump for your property. It's still likely that you have some doubts, so this chapter will clarify the possible viability of other options. We'll explore different decarbonisation options and then the way in which you need to adapt your mindset before embarking on the journey of acquiring a heat pump.

What other options are there to decarbonise our homes?

Installing an air source heat pump in an existing house seems like a big effort. Let's start with the all-important question: *Won't there be a new radical technology just around the corner that will be effortless to install in every home and cheap to run?*

The intention to achieve net zero was enshrined in law in 2008 by The Climate Change Act.[14] The act committed the UK to reducing its greenhouse gas emissions by 80% of the 1990 levels by 2050, with the target subsequently increased to 100%, ie net zero. This overall target has been broken down by sectors, and to meet the targets set for housing – domestic emissions – heat pumps need to be installed at a rate of 600,000 per year by 2028.[15] The current level of installations is at approximately 70,000 per year.

Other than heat pumps, there are a few main ways in which lower carbon emissions can be achieved:

1. Fabric upgrades
2. Hydrogen
3. Biofuels
4. Electric heating

1. Fabric upgrades

A property that is well insulated and has well fitting, thermally efficient windows and doors requires less energy to adequately heat it. I had a conversation with innovative architect Dr Jerry Harrall about the possibility of houses being built with no requirement for heating. He has designed houses that have maintained 21°C indoor temperature without any heating.[16] This possibility is even more utopian than heat pump technology and also further out of reach for the average homeowner seeking to improve their existing property.

Older properties were not built with the same thermal values, that is, good insulation and high-quality windows and doors. Improvements to older properties need to be made by professionals that understand the balance between airtightness, breathability and ventilation to ensure problems of moisture retention, condensation and mould are not created. Improvements to insulation, windows and doors can certainly contribute to energy efficiency. Unfortunately, dogmatically insisting that insulation, windows and doors are upgraded is unhelpful when your boiler needs to be replaced. It causes an unacceptable barrier in terms of effort, time, disruption and capital outlay. Others point out that a heat pump system can be designed to meet the heating requirements that already exist.

2. Hydrogen

As mentioned earlier, converting the domestic gas grid to run on hydrogen is a contentious subject. No trials have been undertaken in the UK, and plans for trials have been shelved until after 2026. Although this is an option favoured by the incumbent mains gas industry, academics say that the transition required of the current gas grid would be prohibitively expensive.

3. Biofuels

The industry behind the production of heating oil is now promoting hydrotreated vegetable oil (HVO) as a replacement for fossil fuels. Does growing fuel make sense in terms of land use, though? HVO is over twice the price of fossil fuel heating oil and is therefore not a financially attractive alternative. Waste cooking oil is being used as fuel, which is positive, but there is only a small quantity available.[17]

4. Electric heating

Many types of electric heating are advertised as energy-efficient and suitable for installation in many situations, but it is important to remember that electric heating can only achieve 100% efficiency. This may sound impressive compared with an 85% efficient boiler, but we laugh at this in the heat pump industry – 500% efficient is what we call good.[18] Seasonal coefficient of performance (SCOP) is the term used for the efficiency of the system. It expresses the output as a figure such as 3.5, which means for every unit of electricity used, 3.5 kW of heat are produced by the heat pump. Or it can be shown as a percentage such as 350%. Both mean the same thing. Any kind of direct electric radiator, storage heater, fan heater or

Tepeo heat battery can only emit the amount of energy drawn from the electricity grid.

A slightly different form of electrical heating is infrared panels, which are useful in occasionally occupied spaces such as churches. This technology heats the person rather than the building, so it has severe limitations both for occupants and the fabric of the building.

If we need to conserve the draw of electricity as we electrify to decarbonise, it is important to keep the use of electricity for heating to a minimum. Heat pumps are not electrical heaters; they use the free warmth from the sun.

In the UK we have high electricity prices; and electricity prices are high compared with gas prices, which is known as the *spark gap*.[19] Currently, many people who have access only to electrical appliances for heating live in fuel poverty. The reality can be people enduring Dickensian conditions with an inadequately heated home, huddling around a small electric radiator with jumpers on.

We expect central heating in the twenty-first century

The image of people huddling around a radiator brings me on to my final topic, about houses previously being built without central heating. We've now had almost two generations with an expectation of central heating. Comfort levels have increased, but this is at the expense of high carbon emissions.

The domestic heating industry has not developed with efficiency in mind. Gas has been cheap, and boiler systems wastefully produce very high temperatures of around 75°C. Did you know that reducing the water temperature in heating systems can reduce carbon emissions, irrespective of the fuel source? All new-build or completely new heating systems are now mandated by building regulations to be designed to work at 55°C flow temperature.[20]

We should be moving forward in a clear and joined-up way. The ideal would be to live in a house needing no heating at all, like those designed by Dr Jerry Harrall. The second-best option is to live in a house not heated by burning stuff, with a central heating system that gives you a comfortable living environment. Elderly people can die in cold homes, while younger people feel uncomfortable and grumpy. Surely that isn't what we should be aspiring to in our technologically advanced world?

Let's come back to my question at the start of this chapter: *Won't there be a new radical technology just around the corner that will be effortless to install in every home and cheap to run?* Sadly, the answer is no – there is no other heating technology that can keep us wonderfully warm and cosy while not burning fossil fuel, wood or other limited resources. Heat pumps harness the energy from the sun, which isn't going to run out any time soon.

Your mindset shift towards heat pumps

It takes some effort to get a heat pump installed, just as it takes effort to make any improvements to your property, but it's easier with a clear vision. If you're installing a new kitchen, you will have a design picture illustrating the final outcome. With a heating system the outcome will be feeling different – more comfortable – in your home. Getting a heat pump is more than replacing a white box on the wall. It is a transition.

Because you are reading this book, you probably don't know what it's like to live with a heat pump system. Before you throw yourself into the process of searching for an installer, I want to share some of my lived experience. The companies you make contact with will ask you what you want, and I want to help you get clear on your answers.

HOT TIP: SEE FOR YOURSELF

Using Nesta's Visit a Heat Pump service, you can visit a heat pump owner to hear their lived experience.[21]

The aim of the change: comfort

The most important outcome of switching to a heat pump is often lost in the noise of media articles and technical jargon of forum posts, and there have even been allegations of propaganda against heat pumps.[22] Living with a heat pump system involves some letting go (of control). This is a positive aspect, though – having an intuitive modern heating system will mean you have one less thing to worry about. My aha moment that led to me writing *Warm Wisdom* is that I'm not at all interested in how my heating system works. You don't need to be either – once your system is set up it should just work; it should keep you warm. It should also cost at least a bit less to run than a gas boiler system.

HOT TIPS: BEING CHILLED ABOUT YOUR HEATING

Irrespective of the amount of research you have done into heat pumps, avoid being dictatorial with installers. Use your knowledge but zoom out and express what you want in general terms. Let me illustrate what I mean about how the relationship with your installer should begin:

- Try to avoid specifying products, controls or system design to the installer. Each company will have in-depth knowledge of the products they offer.
- At the initial meeting, outline what you're trying to achieve, eg *I want to replace my oil boiler with a low-carbon alternative – it's twenty-five years old and keeps breaking down.*

- Allow the installer to be the expert and suggest the best solution to your problem.
- Take a neutral stance – however well-read you are, listen carefully to what is being proposed so you can begin to gauge the credibility of the company.

If you are retrofitting a heat pump, consider your answers to the following questions:

- How important is it to you to have the least possible disruption and fewest radiator changes?
- Is achieving the lowest possible running costs your main priority?

Doing this and expressing your position to potential installers will help them specify and design a system that meets your needs.

Payback

There has been a lot of debate in the media about whether switching to a heat pump is worth the financial outlay, and in 2025 Channel 5 made a documentary on this question featuring my company, R A Brown Heating Services.[23]

Generally, heat pumps are grouped in with other renewable technologies such as solar PV and battery storage, but this isn't a good comparison. It is natural to calculate how long it might take for solar PV or batteries to save you money, taking the initial investment into account, but these types of equipment don't enhance your life at all. They harness electricity for you to use and store, which is useful and satisfying, but nothing changes in your house. I might make an exception only for hot tubs, having witnessed the delight of being able to use a luxury hot tub heated by solar-generated electricity.

A heat pump system provides a physical benefit of comfort – a different type of warm environment than you had with a boiler.

Many installers feel on the back foot, trying to defend what a heat pump has to offer. Because heat pump systems are more expensive than boiler systems, installers feel they need to offer the lowest cost possible, even if that means a low-quality product.

It's important here to consider two points:

- If you're buying a new boiler, do you choose the cheapest make?
- If you're buying a new kitchen or a new car, do you expect a payback from it?

The tabloid press has been full of sensational stories about homeowners being left in the cold due to bodged heat pump installations. There is a largely unreported, hugely positive story about heat pump adoption, though, demonstrated by the satisfied customers we have worked with over the past seventeen years.

My husband Richard Brown likes to use an analogy of the car industry, saying that the heat pump market is similar to the car industry at the start of the twentieth century. Rich people had cars first because they could afford them, and it was some time before almost everyone was able to join them on the roads. Similarly, wealthy people are already confident in heat pump technology – they are happy with the systems and live comfortably in their homes. We're still several years away from heat pumps becoming the norm, but the technology is fully developed, and the industry is beginning to align itself in readiness for mass adoption.

Warm wisdom – key points

- **Decarbonisation options.** You shouldn't wait for a radical, effortless new heating technology – it isn't coming. The UK's legal commitment to net zero by 2050 means we need to ramp up heat pump installations. Fabric upgrades and insulation, hydrogen, biofuels and electric heating are unviable. Heat pumps harness the sun's energy, providing an efficient, low-carbon central heating solution without the need to burn anything.

- **Mindset shift.** When faced with the prospect of choosing the right heat pump and the best installer, it's important that you ignore arguments around payback. Better is to visit another homeowner who has already switched, to give you clarity on what you want and why. You don't need to waste time and effort focusing on specific makes of heat pump – you can leave that to the installer.

PART TWO

FIRST STEPS TO ACQUIRING A HEAT PUMP

THREE
Financing Your Project

Financing a heat pump in the UK can be difficult due to strict regulations and the limited availability of suitable financial products. The prospect of finding the ideal installer for your new heat pump might also feel daunting, especially if you know few people who have already opted for this low-carbon heating technology.

In this chapter I will clarify the main challenges and solutions in gaining financial support.

Finance options for buying a heat pump

This topic is probably the single most frustrating one for me. I would dearly love every British homeowner to be able to purchase a heat pump. Just as we can't all afford a glamorous new kitchen when we want one, though, not everyone has the capital needed to switch to a heat pump when their boiler is on its way out.

It has taken me a long time to understand the difficulty in providing affordable finance for UK homeowners (and landlords) to purchase heat pumps. We have some of the strictest regulations in Europe, set by the Financial Conduct Authority (FCA), which have made it almost impossible to create suitable products to finance domestic heat pumps.[24]

Hire purchase agreements don't work, because a heat pump isn't something you can rent. It would be contentious to remove a heat pump system, so if the instalments were not paid, there would be no way to realistically reclaim the asset. In theory, existing money such as pension pots could be put to use to provide loans at low interest, but this mechanism is currently not available in the UK. The whole area of finance has felt very stuck for at least three years, since the end of the RHI.

Thankfully, though, a handful of innovative organisations are moving into this space. There are some finance options, and it is likely more will be available in the future. Let's look now at the current schemes that might enable you to invest in a heat pump:

- Buying a heat pump via a monthly subscription
- Third-party ownership (TPO)[25]

- Green mortgages
- Grants, 0% VAT and free heat pumps

Buying a heat pump via a monthly subscription

The only company offering this at the moment (to my knowledge) is Fornax Energy. I can't praise these pioneers highly enough, particularly founder and CEO David Leviseur. I am privileged, in my role at R A Brown Heating Services, to support innovators who need to sense check what they are trying to create with business owners in the sector, and this is one that I am excited about.

Fornax have achieved the seemingly impossible – a credible way for people to acquire heat pumps via payment of a monthly fee, while benefiting from the BUS grant and gaining the security of a maintenance and service package for up to twelve years. Fornax have worked hard on the details to make the process flexible and workable. Other advantages of their approach include:

- They work with high-quality manufacturers, as they want your system to last more than twelve years.
- They work with real independent installers around the country. As a consumer, you can approach Fornax to see which installers they work with in your area, or search for installers that are partnered with Fornax.

Founded in 2022, Fornax currently operates on a small scale. They aim to grow their business slowly, working with quality installers rather than trying to achieve volume quickly and potentially compromising the quality of the installations. I hope they do manage to scale with the industry because what they are offering has real value. Monthly payments offer affordability, and in-built servicing and maintenance give the homeowner peace of mind and security.

Third-party ownership (TPO)

TPO is a complex financial arrangement where, instead of you owning the heat pump equipment, there is a kind of hire agreement. Robust contractual arrangements are needed to protect both parties as, in the case of default, removing the asset – the heat pump – is challenging.

Currently, this type of financial agreement is not common because you are required to own the heat pump equipment for eligibility to access the BUS grant, though this requirement might be changed to allow these financial products to come into the market.

Green mortgages

On the face of it, it seems obvious that homeowners should be able to borrow additional money at competitive rates to incentivise their decarbonisation measures. Unfortunately, though, it seems our mortgage sector in the UK is not flexible enough to make this properly viable, and green mortgage products have failed over the last few years. Behind a statistic of low take-up, restrictive terms and conditions exclude many households.[26]

Often, green mortgages are only available if your house is already achieving an energy performance certificate (EPC) rating of A or B. Achieving this rating is quite tough for most retrofit scenarios, but many properties with an EPC rating of C or D could successfully complete a heat pump retrofit. I have also noticed that the additional green borrowing allowances provide insufficient funds to subsidise the required improvements.

As a comparison, homeowners in France have been able to take advantage of the extremely successful 0% interest 'green loan' – éco-prêt à taux zéro (eco-PTZ) – of up to €30,000 for the past ten years. This allows people to upgrade their windows and doors, improve insulation and fit a heat pump system, all via a simple application system though high street banks. It has really stimulated the French domestic heat pump market.[27]

Green mortgage products will come and go over time. I will post updates on new products that I come across, which you will be able to access on the Resources page of my company's website: https://rabrown.co.uk/category/resources.

Grants, 0% VAT and free heat pumps

The government are committed to subsidising heat pump systems by £7,500, potentially until 2030, via the BUS grant. At the time of writing, the UK Government has committed to extending the BUS scheme to provide a £2,500 grant towards the cost of air-to-air heat pumps.[28]

All of the equipment and the installation of renewables, including a heat pump and the required heat emitters, attract 0% VAT, creating an immediate 5% saving. This is due to continue until 31 March 2027.[29]

HOT TIP: DON'T DELAY

I recommend that you don't wait for a miraculous price drop. If your boiler is around twelve years old and you are attracted to a heat pump, plan an installation now.

As you can see from the information above, there are at least some subsidies in place to support you, and there are some finance options coming into the market.[30]

Warm wisdom – key points

- **Financial incentives.** Financial support for obtaining a heat pump is limited in the UK, but there will hopefully soon be additional options. For now, financial incentives include green mortgages, though these often have tough restrictions; government support, including the BUS grant and a 0% VAT rate on heat pump equipment and installation; and TPO. Fornax Energy also provides an innovative solution with a monthly payment plan.

- **ECO4.** Currently homeowners on low incomes can access a range of free upgrades under this scheme. This is due to be discontinued by the end of 2026 with a replacement scheme to be introduced in April 2027.

FOUR

How To Get Started On Your Project

Now that you have carefully considered most of the pre-project planning, it's time to cover the initial installation preparation. This chapter focuses first on retrofit installations, starting with assessing your current heating system and the upgrades that will likely be needed. We'll then move on to the initial considerations and the steps in working together with all the people and companies you have engaged.

The process for new-build installations is slightly more straightforward, but you will still need to be mindful of a range of important aspects, including low-carbon opportunities, coordinating all the contractors and looking after your own wellbeing. All of these points are covered towards the end of this chapter, but let's start with assessing existing properties' requirements.

How old is your existing heating system?

The UK has the oldest housing stock of any European country, with the highest percentage of houses that were built before 1946. This can pose challenges when introducing twenty-first-century technology. Don't despair, though – even stately homes are successfully switching over to heat pumps.

Whatever the age of your house, it is a good idea, before talking to heating contractors, to assess the scale of the upgrades you need to transition to modern heating. We'll start with sections specific to houses of four different eras to help you identify the heating system you will be replacing:

- Houses built before 1985
- Houses built between 1985 and 1994
- Houses built between 1995 and 2010
- Houses built 2010 or later

Houses built before 1985

Typical features of this era of house include:

- Tanks in the loft
- Slow hot water reheat time
- Heating and hot water on at the same time
- No thermostatic radiator valves (TRVs) on radiators

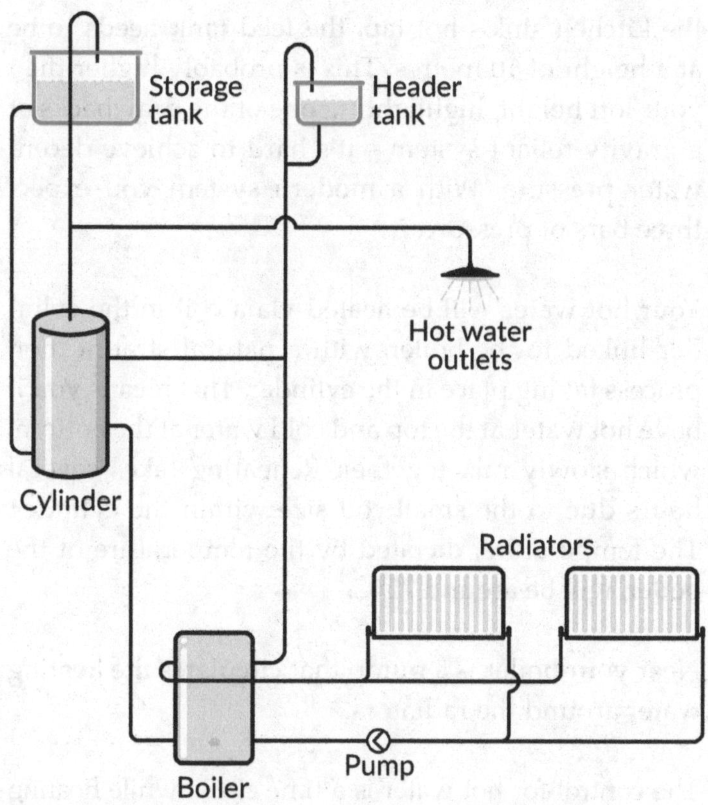

Pre-1985 gravity fed, open-vented system with gravity-heated hot water

Look in your loft – do you see two tanks up there, one of which is a two gallon black tank, about the size of a desktop printer? This is a small store of water to top up the heating system and allow for expansion. A second, larger tank (around 50 gallons) is a hot water feed and expansion tank – a gravity fed, open-vented system that relies on the tank height to provide water pressure at the taps. For one bar of water pressure at the kitchen sink's hot tap, the feed tank needs to be at a height of 10 metres. This is probably higher than your loft height, highlighting one of the drawbacks of a gravity-reliant system – it's hard to achieve decent water pressure. With a modern system you expect three bars of pressure.

Your hot water will be heated via a coil in the cylinder linked to the boiler, with a natural stratification process taking place in the cylinder. This means you'll have hot water at the top and cold water at the bottom, which slowly mix together. Reheating takes several hours due to the small coil size within the cylinder. The temperature, dictated by the temperature of the boiler, will be around 75°C.

Near your boiler is a pump that circulates the heating water around the radiators.

The control for hot water is a time clock, while heating may have a room thermostat for the radiators. Every time the radiator circuit comes on, the hot water is also being heated. Radiators in this era did not have TRVs and were normally single-panel and nonconvecting. Pipework will be copper, usually 15 millimetres in diameter, and it may need to be cleaned by power flushing.

If you have a system like this, it is important to bear in mind that you should upgrade it even if you are having a new condensing boiler installed, meaning the switch to a heat pump is only a small step further.

Houses built between 1985 and 1994

Typical features of this era of house include:

- Pumps on the heating system
- Hot water and radiators that can be switched on independently of each other
- Thermostat on the cylinder
- TRVs and possibly convection radiators

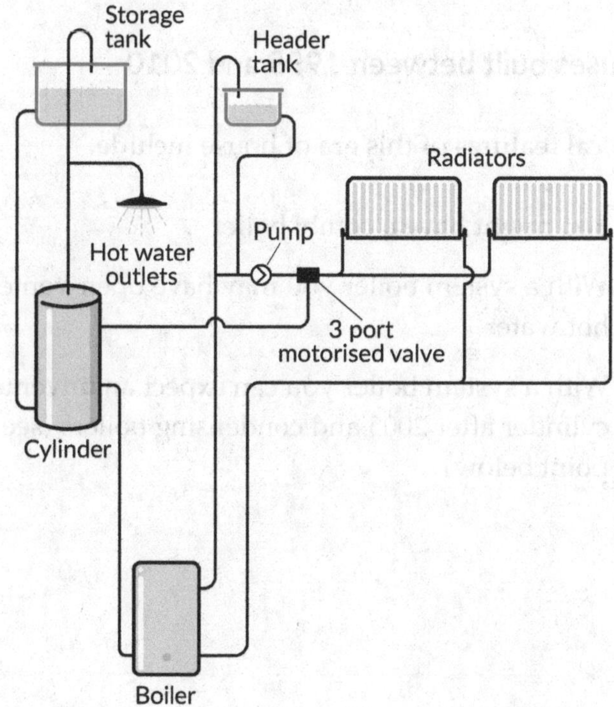

Post-1985 fully pumped vented heating system with 3-port motorised valve (Y Plan)

The hot water supply will typically be the same as in pre-1985 houses. The heating system is fully pumped and is probably in the airing cupboard. There are motorised valves allowing control of the system, with the hot water cylinder and radiators working independently. You have control of hot water temperature via a thermostat on the cylinder. Radiators are still controlled by a room thermostat, but they should be convection radiators with TRVs. Pipework will again be copper and again may need cleaning.

Houses built between 1995 and 2010

Typical features of this era of house include:

- You might have a combi boiler
- With a system boiler you may have open-vented hot water
- With a system boiler you can expect an unvented cylinder after 2005 and condensing boilers (see point below)

This is the era when the combination (combi) boiler became common. This means there is no hot water cylinder, as the boiler produces hot water on demand. Because of this, the kilowattage of the boiler will be higher than that of a system boiler or heat pump.

From around 1995 heating systems started to be sealed, making feed and expansion tanks in the loft obsolete. Unvented hot water cylinders also made the water storage tank in the loft redundant. An unvented system is pressurised via mains water, meaning that all taps provide water that is safe to drink (which it wasn't previously). Unvented cylinders came in after 1995 but weren't common until 2005.

HOT TIP: SHOWER CHECKS

When you switch to an unvented system, you may need to change your showers. Ask the installation company to check this for you.

If you already have a pumped shower with a separate pump, it will be compatible with the change. If your current showers have in-built pumps, though, they will not work with the new unvented system.

After 2005 – condensing boilers

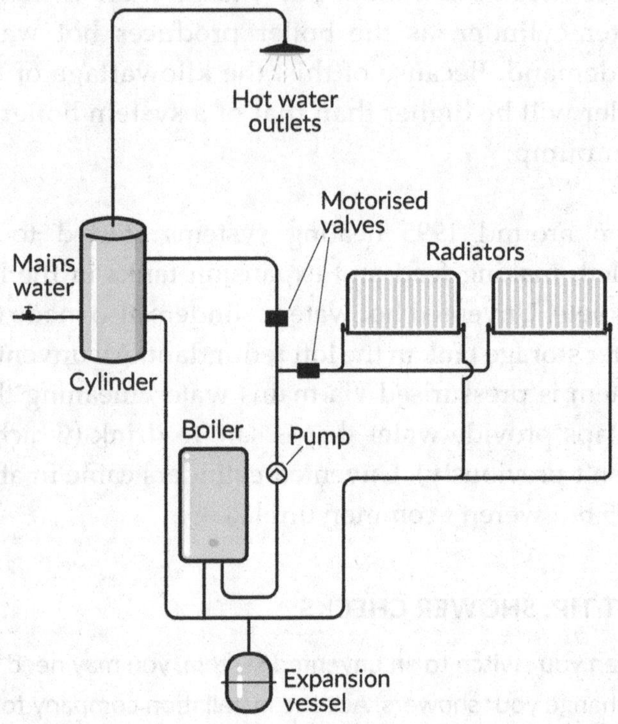

Post-1985 fully pumped sealed heating system with two 2-port motorised valves (S Plan)

A condensing boiler is meant to recover heat from the flue gases and reuse it. Unfortunately, this can only be achieved if the system is designed to work at or below 55°C return temperature.

Returning water from the heating system recovers heat from the flue gases. The advantage is that less heat is discharged from the flue. Homeowners who upgrade to a condensing boiler without assessing their radiators may end up with a boiler that is not able to condense and therefore not work at its best efficiency.

This is also the era when microbore 10 and 8 millimetre pipework in copper and polybutylene plastic became prevalent, and the pipework could be run behind plasterboard walls on new-builds to save installation time. If you have this type of pipework, take extra care to work with an experienced installer as the design work is more complex, but good results are still achievable.

Houses built 2010 or later

This may be the first major heating change for your property. You should have a fully pumped system with unvented hot water or a combi boiler system. Controls will still be similar to pre-1995 systems, with one master thermostat and TRVs. If you have underfloor heating, there may be thermostats in each room. You may also have a separate zone for upstairs radiators.

HOT TIP: AGE IS JUST A NUMBER

Don't forget that if you have an old house, your system could have undergone upgrades at any time. Sometimes the boiler type is changed and the hot water system and the radiators are often left.

Have fun being a heating system detective!

Retrofit installations

When you're planning to install a heat pump, you're making a significant improvement to your home. One of the discouraging factors in making this improvement is that it is not a very visible change like a new kitchen or bathroom. Your comfort experience of living in your home will change, but that is hard to imagine. In this section I want to help you with that.

The work that needs to be done to install a heat pump

Now you know what type of system you've got, let's look at the work involved to change the system. It will be helpful for you first to be able to visualise what the heating engineers will be mapping out in their heads:

1. **Old boiler** – This will need to be removed and disposed of safely unless you are having a hybrid system. For more information go to: rabrown.co.uk / category / resources / warm-wisdom-book-resources.
2. **The ASHP outdoor unit** – This replaces the boiler, and a route from the unit into the house will need to be found and agreed. Ideally, the pipework from the unit will enter the house where the boiler currently is.

3. **The boiler cupboard space** – This can often be used for the new hot water cylinder. If you have a combi boiler or want to change the cylinder position from an upstairs airing cupboard, using the boiler cupboard in this way can be useful.

4. **New equipment** – This includes circulating pumps, diverter valves and expansion vessels, and possibly a buffer vessel or volumiser. The heat pump controller may also be in this cupboard, although it can be located on a wall. You might need a magnetic filter fitted onto an older system retrofit to protect the heat pump from debris in the existing pipework.

5. **Plant room** – A new cupboard or an insulated shed may be needed to house the new equipment.

6. **Existing pipework** – The existing pipework and radiators will be assessed for suitability, and in most cases can be reused.

It also helps to understand what will happen to existing heat emitters and pipework:

- You will have existing pipework running from the boiler position to the radiators.
- Radiators and pipework will be assessed during the survey visit. This involves looking at the size of the pipework and also if radiators can be

increased in size without altering pipework. In most properties existing pipework can be reused. More detailed assessment will be required for microbore pipes.

HOT TIP: COSTS AND COMFORT

Remember that the installer is working to design regulations to balance running costs with ensuring you are kept warm. One of the key areas for decision-making are radiator upgrades (more on that subject later).

The *What if...* exercise

Every house is different, and you know best how your house feels with the way you currently run your heating system. With your new heat pump you will probably be changing to a lower water temperature – a drop from 75°C to below 55°C. If you experiment with different settings before you invite any heat pump engineers in, you'll be able to report your findings to them:

1. Try turning your boiler temperature down to 60°C for a few days – are you still warm enough?
2. Check your radiators – are they all turned on full on the TRVs? If some are on low or turned off, why is that? Make a note to give the heating surveyor this information.

3. Timed settings – if you have your heating set to come on and turn off at certain times, change the settings to have the system run all the time to your set temperature.

The point of this exercise is to simulate living with a low-temperature, open-loop, weather-compensated system. For best results you will set an indoor temperature and allow the heat pump to regulate itself, topping up the heat when needed to maintain your desired temperature. However, on your current system you will have thermostatic controls, which operate in an on/off fashion. This means the controls allow the temperature to drop several degrees below your optimal temperature before turning back on. It also means the level of comfort during your experiment will not be as good as you'll experience when you switch to a heat pump.

While doing this exercise, and when you get your new heat pump, you may have to overcome a fear of your running costs rising dramatically. A car analogy might provide some reassurance. Think about which is more fuel efficient – a car that is driven at the full speed limit but stopping and starting at traffic lights, or a car that is driven at a steady pace throughout its journey. The answer of course is that the car driven at a steady pace is more fuel efficient. It's the same with your heating system, where a lot more energy is required to heat your house up from cold. Because you're used to a high temperature system, you may have the impression of heat continually being blasted in to keep the radiators hot. When the fabric of your house is kept warm, though, only a small amount of energy is needed to maintain the temperature. This is true now, even before you buy a heat pump.

Christine, one of the contributors to *Warm Wisdom*, shared her thoughts on this subject: 'How I view it is that the fabric of the house becomes part of the heating system rather than working against it.'

What you need to know about radiator upgrades

It's common to buy a new boiler without giving a thought to the state or efficiency of your heat emitters, whether those are radiators or underfloor heating. The gas boiler market is competitive, and many installers simply assume homeowners won't be willing to pay for any more work in addition to the boiler change. Contemplating changing to a heat pump may therefore be the first time your radiators have ever been surveyed. With the launch of Heat Geek's ZeroDisrupt system, this aspect is currently a hot topic.[31] The aim of ZeroDisrupt is to deliver an efficient system that is slightly cheaper to run than mains gas, while replacing as few radiators and cylinders as possible. We are currently trialling ZeroDisrupt to see if it delivers as claimed. Results can be variable, which is why the guarantee is critical. As an experienced installer, we are providing feedback to Heat Geek. Other national installers are also beginning to offer similar products.

Understanding what radiators you have

Let's first get familiar with the terminology and find out what radiators you currently have. The most common steel radiators are coded like this:

- K1 (also known as Type 11) – single panel – beneficial to upgrade
- P+ (Type 21) – double panel with single set of fins – better than K1
- K2 (Type 22) – double panel with double set of fins – good enough to retain
- K3 (Type 33) – three panels with three sets of fins – an option offered as an upgrade when switching to a heat pump

Other types of radiators include:

- Cast-iron radiators – these do not convect, but they can work with a heat pump. Their suitability should be assessed.
- Towel rails – white towel rails have a higher output than chrome, and it is helpful to 'oversize' towel rails to allow them to emit heat into the bathroom as well as drying towels.

Finally, if you have any rusty or corroded radiators, it would be beneficial to upgrade these.

HOT TIP: RADIATING VS CONVECTING HEAT

If your radiators feel very hot to the touch, they are radiating heat rather than convecting it effectively into the room.

Convection is the process of pulling in ambient air, heating it and releasing it, which is crucial for distributing warmth efficiently throughout a space. Modern convector radiators are designed to do this much more effectively than single panel or cast iron radiators.

Deciding which radiators might need changing

Think about the cold spots in your house. A number of factors might be causing those:

- A high heat loss area with a lot of glass, such as a bay window, for which there isn't always an easy fix
- An ill-fitting door, which can be improved cheaply by fitting a thick door curtain
- An open fireplace, where you can fit a chimney draft excluder or install a small wood burner into the fireplace

- Areas with no insulation, which are sometimes inaccessible to easily add insulation
- Radiators not working

If it is the heating season, go around your whole house and turn all the radiators on full (you might have already done the experiment in the last section). If they are all working, note if your house feels too warm or just right.

If you still have cold spots, radiators in these areas will need to be replaced with larger ones or different types, for example changing from a P+ to a K2.

HOT TIP: REDUCE, REUSE, RECYCLE

If you have a decent K2 radiator in a cold spot that you want to replace with a K3 or larger K2, measure it and make a note.

The installer may be able to switch that radiator into a different area rather than throwing it away.

Labelling and output of radiators

Take care with information stating the output of radiators. It is often misleading as it gives the output for a high temperature system of 75°C or above.

HOT TIP: DON'T TRY TO CALCULATE YOUR OWN UPGRADED RADIATOR SIZES

It's a complicated process, and your installer will easily be able to provide this information.

If you're self-building or renovating, you're probably used to specifying and buying things independently, but please don't do this with radiators. Even on the website of a major DIY supplies company, the information was woefully inadequate. There was no information related to switching to a heat pump, and they still sell single panel radiators! So you have a general understanding, though, these types of radiators work well with a heat pump:

- **Aluminium radiators** – brilliant at conducting heat
- **Vertical radiators** – a great way to get more heat into a room, as you often have space upwards rather than across
- **K3 radiators** – the popular 'fat' radiators used to replace K1s or K2s
- **Fan-assisted radiators** – push more heat out into the room

HOT TIP: INSIDER KNOW-HOW

If your installer knows a lot about the different types of radiators that can be used with a heat pump, it is a sign they are experienced in low-temperature design.

MCS design standards

One of the MCS design requirements is that radiators are sized to provide adequate heat in a room at a specific outdoor temperature. The heat requirement has to be met on a room-by-room basis rather than as an overall house total.

There are minimum standards set for the efficiency of the system to be compliant with MCS standards. The higher the flow temperature, the less efficient the system will be and the more electricity will be needed to run it. The higher the flow temperature, the fewer new radiators you'll need.[32]

What to do after the heat loss survey

The heat loss survey report will show you the heat load required for each room. It may also suggest a radiator upgrade.

The most straightforward upgrade is where a radiator with a higher heat output but the same dimensions can be installed. This reduces the disruption of altering pipework (if the pipes running to your radiators are 15 millimetres in size). Alternatively, a taller, vertical radiator can be a good option in some places.

When you receive the heat loss survey report, consider two questions:

- Are you happy with the number of radiator upgrades being suggested?
- Are there any options for switching radiators around?

HOT TIP: DON'T BE AFRAID TO QUESTION RECOMMENDATIONS

If you feel you might like to opt for more radiator changes, ask the installer to try inputting different flow temperatures into their software and to reconsider the recommended upgrades.

The lower the flow temperature, the lower the running costs will be.

Remember that radiators installed with your heat pump attract 0% VAT – giving you a 5% saving – until 1 April 2027.

How hot will the radiators feel?

Not very hot. We get a lot of calls from customers saying their radiators aren't working. The first question we ask is 'Are you warm enough?' Usually they say 'Yes'.

When you switch to a heat pump your days of radiator hugging are over. You will experience a comfortable background temperature, but the radiators will be tepid. This is a good thing – it is energy-efficient.

The water temperature is being controlled in a much more sophisticated way. I know it's cold outside if our bedroom radiator is perceptibly warm in the morning.

CASE STUDY: A Low-Stress Retrofit Project

This case study, of one of our retrofit installations, has been included to illustrate that buying a heat pump can be straightforward.

The requirements

This was purely a retrofit installation, with no other improvements being made to the property. The heat loss survey allowed us to assess the sizes of the current radiators. They were quite new, so they would only need to be upgraded if they were not able to provide adequate heat with the lower water temperature system. Calculations completed by our designer showed that only three new radiators needed to be replaced.

Customer wish list

The customers, Mr and Mrs T, told us of four main requirements:

1. To avoid the use of gas, for health and environmental reasons
2. To choose an air source heat pump that was as quiet as possible, because Mrs T is very sensitive to noise, and the couple did not want to cause noise nuisance for their neighbours
3. To retain reusable components of the existing system, as the pipework was adequate and the radiators were quite new

4. To achieve a comfortable living environment, especially as the couple are at home most of the time

The property and motivation

Mr and Mrs T moved house in spring 2023 from a property in a rural area, with storage heaters and a wood burner rather than central heating. Mrs T is very sensitive to many substances and vulnerable to infection; following the Covid pandemic she needs to continually shield. The couple were not keen on the mains gas heating in their new bungalow due to the air pollution it causes.

The bungalow is of typical mid-eighties construction, made of brick with cavity walls.

In addition to their dislike of gas, the couple were also motivated by concern about the climate crisis to reduce their carbon emissions. The sale of their previous property had left them with some capital to spend on improvements to the bungalow, and they had decided on an air source heat pump system.

Finding an installer

Mr T told me he had simply done research on Google and selected three companies to contact. One of the companies didn't provide a quote or estimate, despite having promised to do so. Another provided a very generic guide estimate that didn't have any suggestions of products. My company visited, provided a guide estimate with a choice of heat pump makes, and followed up with enough information and guidance for Mr T to make his decision.

He told me about some friends who had already got a heat pump but were not 100% satisfied with it and were therefore sceptical about anyone being able to straightforwardly hire a good installer. Mr T later told me they were amazed at how easily he had sourced his installation and achieved the result he wanted. This perhaps underlines that you should try not to be put off by people who have had a less than positive experience. Armed with *Warm Wisdom*, it should be possible for you to enjoy having a heat pump installed with little stress.

The installation experience

I asked Mr T if the installation process and amount of disruption were as he expected.

He explained that the installation engineers agreeing to wear face masks had been very reassuring, enabling his wife to continue to shield from potential infections. The couple were also able to decamp to their summer house in the garden during the day while the work was carried out. This was helped by the installation being carried out in September, when the weather was not cold.

Mr T reported that the work lasted for about a week, was in fact less disruptive than he had imagined and was overall very acceptable.

The benefits after a year with a heat pump

Mr T told me he has been happy with the running costs. He has a fixed-price electricity tariff with Good Energy, at a rate of about 26p per kW/hr, and his bills have been at the lower end of what he was expecting. He can't compare running costs with gas as they didn't live with the gas heating for a winter.

He says one of the main benefits is the level of comfort in the house. The heat pump, controlled by weather compensation, provides a lovely, even temperature at all times – a very different experience from the couple's previous house. Living with storage heaters and a wood burner, they were often cold, and it was difficult to keep some rooms warm.

Any drawbacks?

Mr and Mrs T have been concerned at the unit producing noise outside the property, with Mrs T sometimes aware of a slight sound coming from the unit. There have been no complaints from the neighbours, but the couple have wondered if a whole estate of air source heat pumps might be noisy for sensitive people.

Heating nerd status?

I quizzed Mr T about whether he'd become a heating nerd in the process, and he said no. He is considering linking up to the heat pump manufacturer software but feels his system is set up correctly and they are warm and comfortable without high running costs.

Mr T said that, overall, he was very pleased with the experience, feeling they were fortunate to have found a good installer and that the whole process worked well.

Warm wisdom takeaways

- Retrofitting a heat pump is easier if you are clear about the outcome you want to achieve.
- Hiring an independent local installer can be straightforward if you are realistic about the cost.

- Don't be put off by naysayers – there is an ever-increasing number of skilled and experienced installers to choose from.
- If you get all of the factors right – efficiency of the system and electricity tariff – you might achieve even lower bills than you were expecting.
- Even noise-sensitive people can be happy with a heat pump.
- You don't have to become a heating geek – simply nurture the ongoing relationship with the installer.

Buffer vessels

A buffer vessel holds warm water and can reduce on-off compressor cycling (also called short cycling), increasing efficiency and extending system lifespan.[33] Some engineers believe that a buffer vessel combats the negative effect of defrost cycles by preventing cold return flow from reducing emitter temperatures, and that it therefore maintains the comfortable temperature in the house. Other engineers argue against buffer vessels due to cost and space implications. They can also create a small heat loss (approximately 5–10%), because running a buffer vessel requires an additional circulation pump, potentially reducing efficiency by a small amount. Buffer vessels are therefore a contentious subject among engineers passionate about heat pump system design.

Buffer vessels are often useful on retrofit radiator systems. If you are unsure, it will help to listen to the engineer's argument for whether a buffer is a good idea on your system.[34]

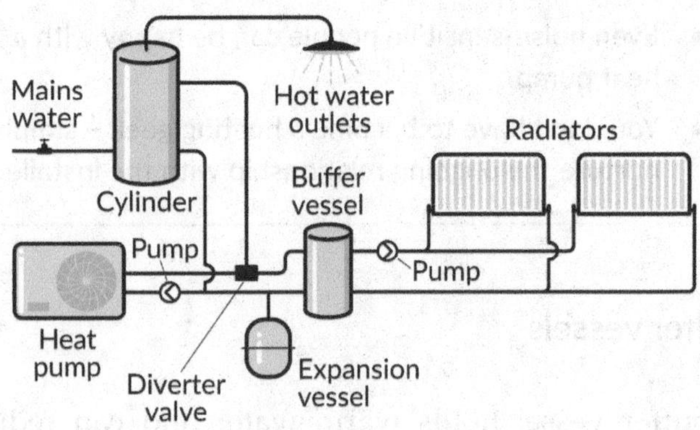

Post-2008 ASHP system with buffer vessel

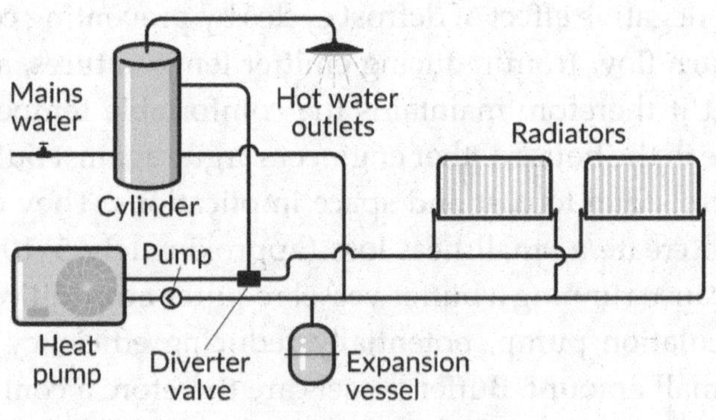

Post-2008 ASHP system with no buffer vessel

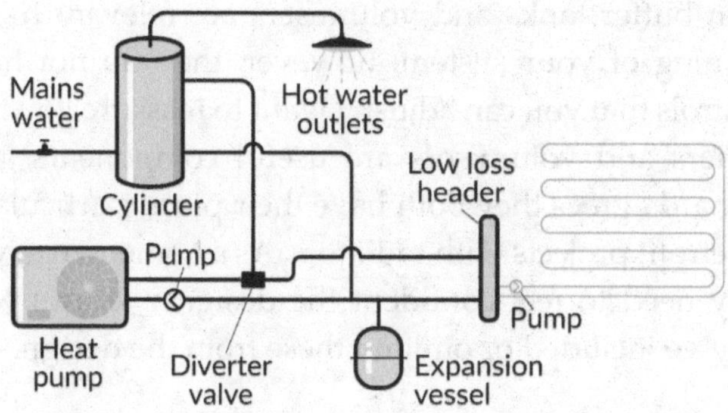

Post-2008 ASHP system with no buffer vessel and underfloor heating

Volumisers

A volumiser is a hydraulic volume booster that prevents short cycling at lower cost and footprint than a buffer tank. We recommend that it is installed on the flow side.[35] Opting for a volumiser rather than a buffer avoids introducing complex hydraulics. Volumisers can moderate cold fluid returns during defrosting and improve comfort.

Engineers who favour buffers argue that a volumiser offers no thermal storage and therefore no buffering of warmth during load variations. The effectiveness depends on sizing and glycol mix, and it is reduced in very low-volume systems such as in a small property with only a few radiators.

Both buffer tanks and volumisers are relevant to the running of your system, however, they do not have controls that you can adjust. I want to reassure you that buffers and volumisers are useful components, and Richard agrees they both have their place, particularly in retrofit projects with radiators. As a homeowner, you only need to feel confident the designer knows why they've included or omitted these from the design.

We don't have a buffer vessel on our system now. We have underfloor heating throughout our ground floor, which acts like a huge buffer vessel. Richard's argument in favour of buffer vessels is that whether a calculated volume of water in a system is actually achieved is dependent on the occupant's behaviour, ie some people keep more radiators turned off or turned down low. The design has been calculated for a fully open loop, and by reducing the volume of water flowing, there is an increased likelihood of a stop-start operation of the heat pump compressor, which is detrimental. Richard feels that a buffer can 'smooth out' the operation of the system beneficially.

New-build installations

The journey to hire a heating contractor is a little different if you are starting from scratch with a new-build, extension or renovation, where there is no existing property to survey and you can't have a discussion on the walkaround.

The good news is that installing a heat pump when you need a completely new system really is a no-brainer. You should be firmly in the mood to future-proof your new (or facelifted) property. It isn't controversial to say that the future will be low carbon, which means:

- You should include microgeneration (solar PV) to add to your feeling of self-sufficiency.
- You can take control of running costs by storing 'fuel' at an off-peak rate, using batteries.
- Particularly with new-builds, you will experience low heat losses as current building regulations require you to build to a high level of thermal efficiency (highly insulated).
- Underfloor heating is usually an easy option, and most people find it really enhances the comfort factor.

HOT TIP: UNDERSTANDING THE BASICS

Read *Beginner's Guide to Eco Renovation* by Judith Leary-Joyce for some wonderful advice on managing your home renovation with an eco-conscious mindset.[36]

When to talk to heating contractors

As long as you have a set of reasonably finalised drawings, it's OK to start approaching companies before you've received planning permission. This might sound counterintuitive, but it's important to speak early to the heating contractor, even before hiring a builder, because the heating firm needs to have an input into the design. The architect doesn't cover this part of the design, and the end client often doesn't fully understand why they need their heating and electrical services designed separately, which means that mechanical and electrical design (M&E) can end up in a no man's land. Some people end up paying a separate M&E designer, but that can end up with them specifying products that don't match up with what the heating contractors actually install. Another drawback is that the heating contractor will have to calculate heat loss and design a system for you if you want to receive the BUS grant. If you're not careful, you can end up wasting money, effectively paying twice. An M&E designer hired by the architect will produce a theoretical specification of products and design that is often not realistic for a contractor to install.

HOT TIP: GO LARGE

Make contact early on, and approach larger heating contractors that advertise design services. They may employ an M&E designer who can work directly with the architect, meaning you won't need anyone else.

What to do when you've found the right contractors

You'll find lots of practical advice in Chapter Five on selecting an installer. Specific to new-build projects, though: it's important to bear in mind that you'll want to build up a constructive, collaborative relationship with your heating contractor. A good place to start is sending them your digital plans and asking for an initial estimate, which will form the basis for further discussions.

If you do begin by speaking to builders, it's worth asking them about heat pump contractors, but make sure you follow the same process of dealing directly with contractors, ie not via the builder. I've spoken to many homeowners who regret not checking the heat pump credentials of their builder's heating contractor.

HOT TIP: FIRST MEETING

If you have the option of having an in-person meeting to discuss the designs and products, this is a great way to see if you feel they are a good fit. Include your architect and/or building contractor at this point.

There is going to be a long gap after the initial meetings and design proposal to the start of the work onsite. Before you get tied up with other decisions, take time to find out all of the services your preferred contractor can offer. Use the following checklist to guide you:

1. If you need MVHR, ask if they offer design and installation of this.
2. Check whether the company offers plumbing too, clarifying that this is just *first fix* (see Definitions of Technical Terms and Jargon section at the end of the book).
3. Ask if they install bathrooms and kitchens – *second fix* (see Definitions of Technical Terms and Jargon).
4. Double-check that they are MCS registered and also registered to provide the BUS grant; this is shown on the MCS website.
5. Talk to them about keeping in touch and about how much notice they need to produce the proposal and contract, then book the work in when you are ready.
6. If you have appointed a builder (or when you do), introduce them to the heating contractor.
7. Ask about electrical work as heat pump wiring is specialist work. The heat pump installer will likely work with an electrician all the time.

HOT TIP: DO YOUR HOMEWORK

Speak to people who have already installed a heat pump. Look at Nesta's Visit a Heat Pump scheme or ask your installer if they have a self-build or renovation customer you can visit.

Clarify the roles

It's important to confirm who is going to manage the project. The builder might offer this service, but you can't assume they will. If you are intending to manage the project yourself, you'll still need an in-depth discussion with the builder about this. If you need a separate project manager, seek out one carefully, ideally by personal recommendation, as quality varies tremendously.

Often building contractors have plumbing and heating firms they routinely work with. Sometimes the builder will try to knock the specialist contractor you've been building a relationship with out of the equation by saying their plumbers can cover everything. If this is the case, be cautious and remember that the heating contractor will have to design a system for you if you want to receive the BUS grant.

In your new-build project, you will very likely need other plumbing work completed such as the installation of bathrooms and kitchens. Make sure all the contracts are clear on where one company's work ends and the other company's begins.

Expect to work with two different electricians – one working alongside the builder and one working with the heat pump installer. Again, it is important that all parties communicate properly so that everything is joined up correctly.

HOT TIPS: TIMING

Make sure you introduce the builder and the heat pump installer to each other in good time. Don't forget you'll need the proposal to be completely repriced and alterations to the design made if anything has changed on the build.

Book a site meeting as early as possible. You need to allow time to sign the contract, pay the deposit and get your project booked in. I recommend allowing at least eight weeks to complete this before the time you'll need the heat pump installer.

We often get calls from people we have only produced a guide estimate for wanting us to be onsite the next week, but that is impossible to achieve.

Keeping a focus on your wellbeing

We've been working on self-build, renovation and extension projects for decades and have seen many extremely stressed customers during that time. It's not surprising – moving house is one of the most stressful things you can do, and building or renovating or extending your house is even more challenging.

As a trained wellbeing professional, I strongly advise that you cut yourself some slack during the project. Try not to have hard deadlines – *We want to be in by Christmas* is a real, detrimental phenomenon. Recognise that there are many external factors that you have no control of such as items being manufactured, tradespeople's availability, and electrical supplies being upgraded (with delays here very common). Keep communication channels open with all of the contractors and suppliers. Above all, remember that it is impossible to run a building project like a military operation, and it will take longer than you first thought.

HOT TIP: BE ZEN ABOUT YOUR BUILD

Recognise you'll be producing more stress hormones than usual and that this will adversely affect your mood and relationships. Take positive action by creating a new routine of exercise, meditation, etc to counteract this.

Warm wisdom – key points

- **The age of your heating system.** If you are looking to fit a heat pump into an existing property, identify the features of your current heating system so that you can assess the scale of upgrades required. The heating systems of most homes in the UK are determined by the year in which the houses were built, although it is likely some upgrading work will have been completed on older properties.
- **Retrofit installations.** While your installer and heating contractor will take care of all

the steps required, it always helps to have an understanding of the work involved, including your old boiler being removed, the best position of the new heat pump, and the existing pipework and new equipment. You will also want to experiment with your current system to get a feel for how the new heat pump will make your house feel.

- **Radiator upgrades in retrofit installations.** It's important to recognise what radiators you currently have to help you know which ones will need to be replaced and whether any of the better ones can be reused. This information will help you to understand and question the heat loss survey report.

- **New-build installations.** It's important to engage early with a heating contractor to ensure that M&E is taken fully into account. Investigate all of the services your heating contractor can supply and make sure they are BUS and MCS registered. You will also need to clarify all contractor roles to allow the project to run collaboratively and smoothly.

PART THREE

WORKING WITH AN INSTALLER, FROM ESTIMATE TO CONTRACT

FIVE

Selecting The Right Installer

This is likely the first time you have embarked on the journey towards installing a new heat pump, so this chapter will provide some practical advice on how to choose and start working with your new heating contractor. You have several options regarding types of installers that will take you on very different journeys, and you may want to explore more than one route.

As with any new project, especially anything related to home improvement, the choice of any contractors will have a significant impact on your satisfaction and experience during the project and on the quality of the outcome. I've therefore concluded this chapter with three case studies to give you real-life examples of how different people made their choices and of their subsequent experiences.

Let's start, though, by exploring the role of the Microgeneration Certification Scheme (MCS).

Introduction to MCS

In the UK our domestic heat pump industry has developed since 2007 with an organisation called MCS at its centre. If you want to know more about MCS, I have included a detailed section in the 'Industry Deep Dives' section at the end of the book.

By working in conjunction with certification bodies, MCS provides standards for installation and a kind of accreditation of installers. One of the main incentives for installers to go through the process of accreditation and regular re-assessment is to give their customers access to government funded grants. At the time of writing, the BUS subsidises most domestic installations by £7,500.

A homeowner only needs to employ an MCS registered installer if they want to claim the BUS grant, which most people do. Unfortunately, MCS registration does not guarantee a high quality installation because the scheme has historically focused on the quality assurance (or paperwork) of the installation company. There is a skills shortage among certification body assessors, who are in some instances not properly qualified to assess the technical quality of the installation.

You need to employ an MCS registered installer or a small installer contractually connected, through an umbrella scheme, with an MCS registered company. This is why additional advice about finding a skilled installer is valuable.

Types of installation company

There are nine types of heat pump installers:

1. **Electrical specialists** – Companies that install a few heat pumps alongside their main business of solar PV and battery storage
2. **Utility companies** – National installers, eg Octopus, E.ON, British Gas (for more information on National Installers, please see Chapter 9)
3. **Fornax Energy** – Online platform that offers alternative routes to buy a heat pump
4. **Online platform umbrella companies** – Umbrella companies, eg Genous Earth, that have an online platform and carry out the design, then subcontract the installation to a local installer
5. **ECO4** – This scheme provides measures for low-income households. It is being phased out and will end in December 2026. It is already

winding down as an end date of April 2026 was announced in November 2025. A replacement scheme is being devised as part of The Warm Homes Plan, with an aim to get a new scheme in place by 2027[37]

6. **Heat Geek** – A company that offers training and the optional follow-on of its own installer registration and guarantee scheme (another type of umbrella scheme)
7. **Air con** – Air-to-air (air con) specialists that also install ASHPs
8. **Manufacturer's umbrella** – Manufacturers that run their own umbrella schemes, where they design the system and train gas engineers to work as subcontracted installers
9. **Independent specialists** – Specialist independent heating installers such as my company

In the table below I've summarised key information to consider about each type of installer.

Installer type	Pros	Cons	Ideal customer
Electrical specialist	Heat pumps run on electricity, so you need a skilled electrician during an ASHP installation. Anecdotally, recent market conditions have enabled many solar PV companies to grow larger. This means they will have back-office support for customers.	It's a good idea to check who is designing your system as the design skills are very different between electrical systems and wet heating systems.	Homeowners that want a full package of solar PV, batteries, electric vehicles (EV) charger and ASHP.
Utility companies	They usually offer a very competitive price. There should be backup if the installation does not meet a minimum required standard.	Their process is disjointed and compartmentalised. They offer a limited range of services, only for certain property types and sizes, and retrofit only. The design temperature may be higher than optimal to reduce radiator upgrades.	Their own electricity customers. Homeowners currently with a gas or oil boiler only needing to change their boiler – not renovating, building, etc.

(cont.)

Installer type	Pros	Cons	Ideal customer
Fornax Energy	They offer a monthly packaged payment option covering heat pump installation, servicing and maintenance for an agreed period. They have a relationship with the manufacturer to ensure the unit is kept in good working order, which reduces worry for the homeowner.	There is a complex, four-way contractual arrangement between Fornax (their financial backers), manufacturer, installer and customer. Fornax are growing sustainably at present and may now have full national coverage of installers.	Any homeowners who do not have the capital for their installation. People who intend to live in their property for the duration of the agreement (there are options if you move). People replacing a heat pump and cannot access the BUS grant.
Online platform umbrella companies	You are likely to go on a journey with this type of company because they have a platform that starts you off on the design options available. If you like the information they provide on decarbonising your home, you may want to continue through the process.	These types of companies rely on subcontractors to carry out the installation to the agreed design.	Homeowners attracted to research using tech rather than calling a local company.

Installer type	Pros	Cons	Ideal customer
ECO4 (ends in December 2026)	You can get solar PV, insulation and a heat pump installed at no cost to you if you are a homeowner or private tenant with a low household income, of under £31,000.	You must have an EPC of D or lower. It is challenging to get a good-quality install; you should not accept a heat pump installation that takes only two days. Budgets are tight, meaning installers are very time-pressured and probably don't always use fully qualified staff.	Low-income households, including retired people.
Heat Geek	They are a well-known national brand with well-regarded training and some of the best heat pump engineers in the UK. They have innovative technology and monitoring of past installs.	Completion of their training alone doesn't guarantee a competent installer. You need to check that the installer is registered as a Heat Geek-verified to access the guarantees.	Able-to-pay homeowners.

Installer type	Pros	Cons	Ideal customer
Air con	This is a good option if you want an air-to-air system. Specialists are fully trained on refrigerants.	Refrigerant engineers are not trained to design the wet heating system needed for ASHPs, so you need to look for a larger, multiskilled firm.	Able-to-pay homeowners.
Manufacturer's umbrella	You are a direct customer of the product manufacturer, which is beneficial for aftersales support. As long as they maintain a full network of installers, the service should be good.	Pricing may be expensive.	Able-to-pay homeowners with all types of property.
Independent specialists	HP specialists are more highly skilled as design is critical. They tend to run on old-fashioned word-of-mouth recommendations.	Very small firms can appear difficult to communicate with as they often work on one install at a time, fitting in surveying and paperwork in between. Larger firms can be expensive due to the need for a skilled back-office team.	Able-to-pay homeowners. Often also commercial projects, eco builds, small high-end developments, rural estates (halls or stately homes).

In general, remember that you get what you pay for. Paying more should mean you experience less stress, more control and better aftercare.

How to find an installer

As explained above, you need to hire an MCS installer (or one that works with an umbrella provider) to access the BUS grant.

The best place to start is by carrying out a geographical Google search. Something like Air Source Heat Pump Installers in XYZ town or near me. I wish I could advise you to go directly to the MCS website. Even though MCS have recently re-launched their website the installer search is still very poor. I've been complaining to MCS's helpdesk about it for years.

The main problem lies with the way most installers – even small companies – are listed on the MCS website as working in all of the areas of the UK. For example, I have asked MCS to ensure my company appears only in searches for the eastern region, and for us to be found in searches of all of the towns across Norfolk, but this has not been implemented. Using the MCS website to find an installer can therefore feel like looking for a needle in a haystack, which makes this section even more vital. I recommend you use the MCS website only to double-check the registrations of an installer that you've already found.

HOT TIP: FIND AN INSTALLER CLOSE TO YOU FIRST

Avoid starting your search with the MCS website, as it gives unreliable results.

Worked example of a local installer search

For this example, I've pretended I live in the village of Waltham on the Wolds in rural Leicestershire. I chose this place at random and don't know any heat pump installers in Leicestershire. I have not contacted the companies I've selected but am including their real names so that you can take a look for yourself as a practice exercise for your own installer search.

I googled 'Heat pump installers Leicestershire' and zoomed in on the map view. Two companies came up nearest to my chosen village:

- **Mumford and Sons**

  Their website is dominated by gas and oil services. I would not contact them on the basis that heat pumps are not currently their core business. Considerable additional training and skills are needed to transition to heat pump installation. I want to be sure the company I choose is fully experienced and competent.

- **Earth NRG**

  I would put this company on my shortlist because:

  - The website is dominated by heat pumps and other renewable products.
  - The website includes details of real people, with apparently two directors.
  - They appear to be a small company but specialists in renewables.
  - Google reviews are all five-star. Although there are currently only seventeen, they include personal glowing reviews.
  - Earth NRG offers a full range of services that would be needed by a homeowner upgrading their property: MVHR, underfloor heating, solar PV, battery storage and high-quality heat pumps. I define high-quality products as those made by specialist manufacturers that don't predominantly make boilers or air conditioning, or other electronic products, but are known in Europe as dominant heat pump manufacturers.
  - Accreditations are prominently displayed, including logos for MCS, Heat Geek, Home Insulation and Energy Systems Contractors Scheme (HIES) Consumer Code and NAPIT (National Association of Professional Inspectors and Testers, certification body).

- After some experimentation with the MCS website search, I discovered that searching by town can work reasonably well. It even shows how many miles away the installer is located. I chose Grantham for this example. I found Earth NRG listed sixth on the MCS directory.
- Searching for Waltham on the Wolds on the Heat Geek website, Earth NRG came up instantly as the top entry, geographically nearest at only ten miles away. As explained in the hot tip below, this firm has Heat Geek verified accreditation, having passed additional checks. They pay a monthly fee to Heat Geek, and their installations are covered by performance guarantees and are monitored.

HOT TIP: HEAT GEEK-VERIFIED INSTALLERS

Double-check that an installer comes up on the Heat Geek website. Heat Geek have recently scrapped their map function and now list only fully verified installers. Some installers who have trained but not been verified may still be advertising their association with Heat Geek, but Heat Geek are tightening up their listings to protect their quality and the companies paying the monthly fee to them.

Heat Geek search results also included:

- **Holme Plumbing and Heating**

  I want to include this second Heat Geek verified installer for balance. It is also important to pay attention to personal word-of-mouth recommendations, for example by a local builder. Sometimes it is worth contacting a very small firm if you have some evidence that they might be good. In the absence of a personal recommendation, I'd be likely to trust Holme Plumbing and Heating because they are registered as Heat Geek-verified and have five-star Google reviews. I'm therefore throwing this in as a wild card!

My search on the MCS website brought up other companies, two of which I discarded immediately for reasons such as no website, an outdated Facebook page and them apparently not being heat pump specialists. I did, however, uncover the following two companies, which I added to my shortlist:

- **Geo Green Power**

  I kept this company on my shortlist because they:

  - Are located twenty miles away
  - Seem a decent sized company, with the website showing a big team photo and stating that they employ seventy people

- Show photos on their website of commercial PV but also a lot about heat pumps, including photos of a variety of makes of heat pump and case studies
- Show real people on their website, including a photo of their heating installation manager
- Also install ground source heat pumps – a sign that they should be technically skilled
- Display accreditations on their website home page – MCS, Renewable Energy Consumer C (consumer protection), NICEIC (certification body), CHAS, ISO

- **Heat Centre Renewables**

  I shortlisted this company because they:

  - Are based sixteen miles away
  - Feature quality heat pumps prominently on their website
  - Talk about design services

Further investigations

Having created a strong shortlist of three or four companies, you will need to speak to each of them to find out more information. I recommend using the questions given in the table below, where you will also find satisfactory (green-light) and questionable or poor (amber- or red-light) answers.

Questions to ask	Green-light answer	Amber- or red-light answer
Do you specialise in domestic heat pump installations?	*Yes. We are BUS-registered, and we install in all types of property.* *Tell me what you're looking for...*	*Yes, but we mainly install for housing associations and do solar PV.*
What is your initial process? (For example, do they begin with a guide estimate or site survey?)	(They describe a clear journey. Refer to the previous section outlining the usual steps.)	(If they can't really answer clearly, this might show lack of experience.)
Can I speak to one of your customers and perhaps visit an installation?	*Yes. What type of property do you have, so I can match you up? Also, some of our installations are registered on the Nesta Visit a Heat Pump scheme.*	*I'm not sure if I can arrange that.*
Do you charge for the heat loss survey?	(Charges are often around £350 to £500. Refunding the fee if the job is won is quite usual too.)	

(cont.)

Questions to ask	Green-light answer	Amber- or red-light answer
How far ahead are you booking work at the moment?	*Around four to six weeks.* (This would be normal.)	*Six months.* (If you want a retrofit, this is probably too long. If you're a self-builder, you need to bear their diary in mind.)
Do you offer aftersales support and servicing?	*Yes – we offer extended warranties,* annual servicing, service plans to spread the cost of servicing. We are also service* [ie maintenance] *partners for XYZ heat pumps.* *(Available if the installer has completed training with the manufacturer and is a VIP with them.)	*No – we don't have a local servicing team. You can get servicing through the manufacturer.*
Self-build question: Do you offer plumbing, underfloor heating (design and install), MVHR?	*Yes – in addition to heat pump services, we offer first fix plumbing* [see Definitions of Technical Terms and Jargon], *a full range of underfloor heating solutions and MVHR design and install.*	*No – we only install ASHPs and cylinders and do radiator upgrades.*

HOT TIPS: WHAT TO LOOK FOR AND WHAT TO AVOID

- Look for a local company. If you are in a rural area with poor roads, you need someone no further than thirty to forty miles away.
- Look for an MCS and BUS registered company or a Heat Geek-verified installer.
- It can be easier to deal with a larger firm with a back office. There are many tiny firms that are competent, but it may take more perseverance and patience on your part to know whether they are competent.
- Avoid companies that seem to have a sales team that are not technical – you could end up with a disjointed and unsatisfactory experience.
- Avoid, or tread carefully, if background research reveals lots of name changes and not much trading history. Dubious practices occur in the construction industry, with firms liquidating then starting up again with new names – a red flag for customers, suppliers and other contractors!

Disclaimer

I have based my advice in the examples above on installation firms found via only a brief internet search and used these companies for illustration purposes only. I have no knowledge of the actual competence levels and capabilities these companies may have, and their websites, services and reviews will change over time.

CASE STUDY: How It Can Help to Work With a Smaller, Independent Specialist

This is a story about how our own journey started, which might help you to spark a conversation with a potential installer.

Our company first entered the heat pump market after Richard was inspired when working on an award-winning innovative self-build in Suffolk, Sliding House.[38] He quickly realised that heat pumps instead of oil boilers would be ideal for rural properties with UFH. He realised this was our future.

A number of skills made it possible for R A Brown Heating Services to become an industry pioneer:

- Our abilities and experience in heating system design
- Our recognition that UFH and heat pumps go together perfectly as they are both lower temperature technologies
- Our confidence in speaking to heat pump manufacturers and attend their training
- Our belief in the technology, enabling us to sell it to customers

Installer as trusted expert

Richard first heard from a couple following a personal recommendation from a local builder. Laurie and Kathy were intending to renovate a bungalow as their retirement home, and they wanted the refurbishment to be as green as possible. They were planning to install solar PV and were interested in other low-carbon technologies.

Richard suggested installing an air source heat pump. They were completely unfamiliar with the technology, but they were particularly interested when Richard said he was just about to install one at our house. Because we trusted the technology to heat our family home, it seems they could trust that it would work for them too. They went ahead and became very early adopters.

Laurie and Kathy's heat pump is still going strong. They are still raving about the comfort and low running costs they've enjoyed for the last seventeen years and the carbon they haven't produced. You can find further information on the project on our website: https://rabrown.co.uk/projects/revisit-first-air-source-heat-pump-installation.

Peers as trusted experts

With Nesta's Visit a Heat Pump scheme, homeowners can now help each other on the journey. Our house is registered on the scheme, and we're happy to share our knowledge and experience on neutral territory rather than at our business premises, even if doesn't end up in a lead for our company.

Having a heat pump installed requires considerable effort and time for all parties involved, so building a relationship of trust with your installer is important. Ask them about their personal journey with heat pumps and if people at the company have heat pumps in their own homes.

Warm wisdom takeaways

- It doesn't matter what size the installation company is – it's their commitment to heat pumps that counts.

- Find out what their story is, especially why they got into heat pumps.
- Word-of-mouth recommendations can be very beneficial, especially if you can find someone local who has strong experience in heat pumps.

Look at Nesta's Visit a Heat Pump scheme to see real-life examples.[39]

CASE STUDY: Paul Eastwood – Questions I Now Know to Ask When Finding an Installer (and a Lesson in Time-Wasting, Frustration and Then Serendipity)

Paul Eastwood is a homeowner and sustainability professional, living in Glasgow, who has documented his experience of buying a heat pump in LinkedIn blogs. He has kindly agreed with us sharing the following case study describing his personal experience in selecting an installer, told in his own words.

It wasn't easy securing quotes. Is it ever? I contacted a number of installers via the Energy Saving Trust Installer Finder.[40] (Please note this is only available in Scotland.)

Some never replied, while others did and either said my home wasn't suitable for a heat pump or only offered a hybrid system, a heat pump and gas boiler combined. After many months of searching, I eventually secured a quote for a 17 kW heat pump, about the largest on the market. That didn't seem unreasonable – my home is old and not strongly insulated – but I wanted a second opinion.

In a rare moment of internet serendipity, an exchange on LinkedIn led me to a company outside of my original search zone. They conducted a full heat demand assessment of my home, seemed very competent and knowledgeable, and proposed a smaller 13.5 kW unit. Why was this?

As we don't have the useful Energy Saving Trust Installer Finder in England or Wales, I've devised my own method for you to search for a local installer:

Question 1: What size heat pump does my home need?

Heat pumps are sized, as I learned, to meet peak heating demand, the level of heat required on the coldest day of the year. Glaswegians will probably disagree, but the city has a relatively mild climate. It doesn't often snow, and when it does, it doesn't last for too long. The outside temperature used to determine peak heating demand was -4°C, which is at the lower end of the temperatures I've experienced since living here. The inside temperatures were set to 21°C for all living rooms, 18°C for all other rooms, and 22°C for the bathroom. This means that the heat pump has to generate sufficient heat to deliver up to a 25°C rise in temperature, or a little less if looking at the average temperature for the house.

The design temperatures are warmer than we usually keep our house but installers design around the house rather than personal usage following MCS guidance.[41] For homeowners to receive the heat pump financial support currently available in the UK, installers need to be MCS certified and follow MCS guidance.

Based on the design temperatures, the size of my home (approximately 160 square metres), and assumptions made around insulation levels and airtightness, peak heat demand was estimated to be 9.5 kW – far lower than the first quote I received.

To recap:

- Quote 1 was for a 17 kW heat pump for a peak demand of 14 kW
- Quote 2 was for a 13.5 kW heat pump for a peak demand of 9.5 kW

Why the big difference in the estimates? Two main influencing factors are the levels of insulation and airtightness. The second quote assumed a higher level of airtightness, based on experience of fitting heat pumps into older homes like mine that had been modernised, and it also assumed a higher level of thermal performance from the uninsulated sandstone walls. This resulted in a lower estimated peak heat demand and a smaller heat pump.

To give a sense of the impact of insulation: not long before the heat pump was installed, I upgraded the windows in two rooms from double to triple glazing. These measures brought the peak heat demand down from 9.5 kW to below 9 kW.

The design also recommended upgrading six of the thirteen radiators to larger units, and for an additional radiator in the main living room as there was no space to upgrade the existing one. Crucially, the pipework was assessed to be just about adequate, avoiding the need for any upgrading and all of the disruption and additional expense that would have caused (phew).

Author comment: This is an area that causes understandable confusion, with the different design calculations that can be applied. It is impossible to be 100% sure of whose estimate is most accurate. I would advise not getting stressed by the numbers – assess the installers on other factors, including their abilities to clearly discuss the reasons for the differences.

Question 2: How efficient is the heat pump?

If you care about energy costs, efficiency is crucial. Today's energy prices mean that gas is around three to four times cheaper than electricity, so a well-designed heat pump delivering around 300–400% efficiency can keep a home just as warm as gas for around the same energy costs, and it can even generate savings at higher levels of efficiency.

Heat pumps are not all made equally, so check the efficiency of the unit and ask the installer why it's being recommended over others. You can also find technical details of all MCS certified heat pumps on their website.

Author comment: While I agree that not all heat pumps are made equally, the efficiency of the system is equally important. This relies in part on the water temperature it is designed to run at while meeting 100% of your heat requirement.

Question 3: How will the heat pump be controlled?

In a complete facepalm moment, I didn't even think about asking this question until the day the installation was finished and the van drove away (the handover process was not optimal).

Like many households, our previous gas combi was operated by a wireless indoor thermostat that allowed different temperatures and times to be set. The heat pump had no indoor thermostat, only an outdoor thermometer and a control panel fitted in the 'plant room', as the installers called it. This was essentially the cupboard where the new hot water cylinder, water circulation pumps and expansion vessels were sited – everything needed in addition to the heat pump unit itself.

The installers should also explain the controls that will come with the heat pump, where they might be sited, and whether there are options to increase accessibility, such as apps and web applications. If they don't explain, push for answers.

Author comment: This reminds me of horror stories where homeowners have been asked if they wanted the weather compensation turned on, and they replied no because they didn't know what it was!

Question 4: How will the heat pump look when installed?

Personally, I think aesthetics matter, and some heat pumps are – at least in my view – nicer looking than others. If the unit is visible, you might want to consider choosing a model that you like the look of. Think about size also and imagine it in the location where it will be installed. Some units have double fans to generate higher heat output, and these will be far more of a visible presence.

My heat pump offers the heat output I need from a single fan, whereas other models would only deliver the heat output from a double-fan unit. This is part of the reason why the installer recommended the model they did, as the unit is quite visible from both inside and outside of my home. It is, though, a relatively large single-fan unit, and it has taken a little while to get used to having a large appliance in our back garden. Now I hardly notice it. Visual impact is also a small price to pay when compared with having a gas-free home and lower energy costs.

Author comment: I have the same make of heat pump at my house as Paul, so I don't completely disagree, though I feel aesthetics can't always be the most important factor. Choosing the best installer is more important – do choose a position you're happy with. Oil tanks are ugly but acceptable in rural settings, and you'll learn to love your heat pump even if it isn't beautiful. As an aside, we have had quite a few heat pumps wrapped, usually in a stylish carbon grey, but you could have almost any design or colour.

Warm wisdom takeaways

- Finding an installer: Securing quotes was difficult. The first quote for a large 17 kW unit was based on a flawed heat demand estimate. A second installer, found by chance, proposed a more accurately sized 13.5 kW unit after a thorough assessment of the property's insulation and airtightness.
- System sizing: Heat pumps are sized for peak demand on the coldest day. The second installer's estimate was lower because it correctly accounted for the home's insulation and a higher degree of airtightness.
- System controls: Paul was surprised to find no indoor thermostat, as the system is controlled by an outdoor thermometer and a controller in the

plant room. I feel it's crucial to discuss controls and options like weather compensation early with the installer.

- Aesthetics: The visual impact of the unit matters. Paul chose a single-fan unit for a cleaner look. I feel choosing the best installer is even more important than selecting the most beautiful unit.

HOT TIPS: GO CLOSE TO HOME

- Choose a geographically local installer so you can get setting tweaks, and ask if there is a follow-up visit
- Do the *What if... e*xercise in Chapter Four – play with your system
- Ask early in the process about weather compensation.

CASE STUDY: Mixed Initial Experiences in Finding an Installer

Many people who feel motivated to install a heat pump are recent retirees, often with a desire to decarbonise and take control of their running costs. They know they will be living on a smaller fixed income but have some capital to spend on improvements that will ultimately lead to lower household bills.

Chris and Terry wanted to go gas-free. Chris is very enthusiastic to reduce carbon – she is an eco-champion at her local church, encouraging others to recycle and reuse, and to reduce carbon in every way possible.

Details of the property

Chris and Terry's house is a 1972 self-build timber frame bungalow, with 25 cm of loft insulation and twenty-year-old double glazing. The construction is stud walls with 5 cm of old fibreglass and a 5 cm cavity to the outer brick wall, with no cavity wall insulation. It was not a modern or seemingly ideal property to retrofit.

The journey to buy a heat pump

The couple explained that their son had installed an ASHP two years earlier. This provided firsthand experience that the technology worked. Chris's husband Terry used to be an engineer by profession (not a heating engineer), and this increased their confidence to assess potential installers and ask relevant questions until they found a company that was offering what they wanted.

Their experience of quotes and visits from potential installers

Chris and Terry sought a quote from a local engineer but found him inflexible. His design included all new radiators, but the couple wanted to switch some of their relatively new radiators around rather than buying a whole new set. The design they received specified that underfloor plastic pipes would need to be replaced with copper, requiring the floor to be lifted.

There were further setbacks in that some companies visited but then failed to provide an estimate or a quote.

Finally, a very small company run by two brothers attended for a site visit. They listened to what the couple wanted and talked everything through in a more collaborative way. They were prepared to switch some radiators around, and they came across as credible and communicated well.

Outcome after installation

Once a satisfactory contractor was identified, the installation went smoothly. Chris and Terry also have solar PV and battery storage (which are especially beneficial during the winter). The couple report that their running costs would have been less than with gas, even without solar panels and batteries. They benefit from using a time-of-use electricity tariff to reduce running costs, and these are not available with gas or oil systems. Chris says, 'Solar PV and batteries are the icing on the cake rather than essential for making a heat pump good value.'

Christine says, 'We're still very happy with the system, and it's very efficient.'

They shared their 2024 usage data (with rounded figures), without the distraction of special tariffs:

2024 data

- Import (of electricity) for year: 2,500 kWh
- Consumption: 4,000 kWh (plus EV charging: 500 kWh)
- Generation: 3,000 kWh
- Export: 1,000 kWh
- In twelve months, the heat pump used 1,500 kWh electricity and delivered 7,500 kWh heat
- Heating cost for the whole of 2024 was £180. It would have been £360 for the year if we were using full-cost electricity

- Average: 125 kWh per month, or £31 at 25p per kWh

Note: The heat pump was installed in the second week of January 2024, so this year energy consumption might be higher.

In January 2025 Chris and Terry used 450 kWh total – 30% of all 2024 heating.

Average use in January was 13.8 kWh per day, with 25.6 kWh (highest use) on the coldest day and 22.4 kWh on the adjacent day. At 25p it would have been approximately £110 for all of January 2025, but only January was particularly cold.

Summary

The new system is delivering on comfort and giving Chris and Terry peace of mind that they are reducing their carbon footprint by avoiding reliance on fossil fuels.

Warm wisdom takeaways

- Don't listen to detractors saying only modern properties are suitable for a heat pump.
- Don't feel you have to undertake a significant fabric improvement project before getting a heat pump installed.
- Keep searching until you find an installer who is listening to what you want to achieve.
- Buying a heat pump can be straightforward and stress-free.

Chris pointed out that their installer does not have impressive marketing or website, so it's worth talking to very small companies as potential installers.

Warm wisdom – key points

- **Engaging an installer.** It is vital that you spend time carefully investigating potential installers. You also need to keep an eye on the bigger picture, including installation and aftersales, rather than focusing purely on pricing, and remember that the offerings from national companies can change at any time.
- **MCS.** Any installer you consider needs to have MCS accreditation, which stipulates installation standards and enables installers to give customers access to the BUS grant.
- **Installer options.** There are nine types of heat pump installers, and choosing the type that is best for you will depend on a number of factors, including the size of your property, the complexity of your project and your financial position. Each type has pros and cons, and your experience with a large utility company, for example, will be very different from the service of an independent specialist.
- **Finding an installer.** The MCS website lists all MCS registered installers, but their website search function isn't flawless. Other search functions include general internet searches and Heat Geek's database of verified installers. It's important to create a shortlist, noting points for each installer, not least their familiarity with and expertise in heat pumps, and that they are a BUS and MCS registered company or Heat Geek verified.

SIX

Overview Of A Typical Customer Journey

Your choice of installer will influence the rest of your journey to obtaining a heat pump, starting with your initial inquiry. For example, utility or nationwide installers generally have a highly segmented process, with different people covering each step. Independent installation companies vary in size, but you should expect some continuity and real people actually talking to each other to deliver your job. Meanwhile, if you opt for a Heat Geek registered installer, there will be a structure and organisation behind the engineer you are dealing with, including registrations, certification and guarantees. This is only the case, though, if they are a verified and registered Heat Geek installer, ie with the highest level of training. Not everyone who has trained with Heat Geek is registered in this way, so it is important to check.

In this chapter I will give you an overview of the process you'll experience leading up to the final contract stages, including important points to be aware of at each stage.

A typical process, from inquiry to contract

I have based the following example mainly on our own sales process, to give you a realistic idea of the steps involved in obtaining a heat pump. You will see some differences in the process for retrofit and new-build projects, but both follow five steps:

- Step 1: Initial inquiry and guide estimate
- Step 2: Heat loss survey or specification meeting
- Step 3: Detailed proposal
- Step 4: Proposal agreement
- Step 5: Agreement and contract

Step 1: Initial inquiry and guide estimate

Retrofit: Don't be perturbed if you can't speak to a technical salesperson immediately. There may only be one technical salesperson, who will often be out of the office (if the company is even large enough to have an office). Beginning your inquiry with email correspondence is fine, but I recommend also arranging to speak with the salesperson, giving you a better feel for how they work and what they offer.

Many firms can create a guide estimate instantly from an energy performance certificate (EPC), and you can provide some additional information verbally if they use modern software. Other companies may email a self-survey questionnaire for you to complete and return, while some firms will book a site survey visit straight away. See further information on this step of the process below.

New-build, extension or renovation: Because you have only design drawings, it normally takes longer (up to two weeks) for a guide estimate to be produced than for a retrofit. The detailed information has to be uploaded to software. The upside is that, once this has been done, the heating requirements should be accurate for both the estimate and the proposal.

Step 2: Heat loss survey or specification meeting

Retrofit: If the initial guide estimate meets your expectations, the next step is a heat loss survey visit, for structural data about your property and information about your existing heating system to be gathered. This takes around three hours and is sometimes a chargeable appointment, often with a refund of the fee if the company carries out your installation. Most companies will arrange the survey visit within two weeks if you want to continue the journey with them.

New-build, extension or renovation: You will be offered an appointment to discuss the project, often with physical plans, using displays to show the plant room space required. Sometimes an architect or project manager will attend this meeting too. Not all installers have premises to host this kind of meeting, so they may visit you instead for a detailed discussion of your requirements. This appointment could be within a couple of weeks after the guide estimate.

Note: See the 'New-build installations' section in Chapter Four for further information.

Step 3: Detailed proposal

The data is entered into specialist software, heat requirement is calculated, and a proposal with specification and prices is produced. Expect this step to take a few days.

Step 4: Proposal agreement

You should expect to be offered a call to discuss the proposal details. An experienced installer will readily make amendments to the design or products being offered.

Once agreed, the final proposal should contain MCS documentation and BUS grant information, including a clear payment schedule, in addition to a contract detailing products and services.

Step 5: Agreement and contract

Once the proposal (contract) is signed and a deposit is paid, the job can be booked into the installer's calendar. Ask about the lead time, as it can vary considerably. Many companies will be booking six to eight weeks ahead.

With retrofit projects all these steps can be completed in less than a month. With self-build projects there is usually a long gap between the initial proposal and the final proposal being signed. Several revisions and repricing are likely, and lots of checking in and back and forward is the norm.

HOT TIPS: DOS AND DON'TS IN THE CONTRACT PROCESS

- **Do** ask to speak to a technical salesperson and tell them your story rather than getting bogged down with emails.
- **Do** accept a guide estimate – quickly produced – as a starting point. Discuss this to begin relationship building.
- **Don't** disregard a company that doesn't offer you a free site survey visit straight away.
- **Don't** 'dictate' based on your previous research. Instead, ask questions and listen.

The Heat Geek process

The following steps are clearly shown on the Heat Geek website:[42]

- Step 1: Immediate estimated price based on the information you enter into their online calculator
- Step 2: Within a month, a design consultation at your home
- Step 3: Proposal (no timescale given)
- Step 4: Installation, within about three months from the start of the process
- Step 5: Support, making sure you're comfortable and tweaking the settings based on your feedback

They also have ZeroDisrupt, a new service for retrofit where no home improvements are being completed and where the homeowner hopes to install a heat pump with minimal upgrades to their system. What is now described as Black Label is the normal bespoke design system for all other properties.

The Octopus Energy ASHP installation process

Starting with the Octopus Energy website, the installation process runs as follows:[43]

- **Online quote.** You enter your postcode and property details online for a preliminary quote.
- **Home survey.** A specialist conducts an in-home survey to create a tailored quote for a bespoke system.
- **Prepare for installation.** You pay a deposit to secure your slot, with Octopus claiming the £7,500 BUS grant on your behalf.
- **Installation.** One team handles design, plumbing, electrical work (though I have heard that the design is completed more centrally). Standard installation includes ASHP, cylinder, radiators, pipework and electrical connections.
- **Post-installation.** Waste and rubbish are removed and recycled where possible. The lead installer reviews controls with you, checks you're happy and supports you with your new system.
- **Aftercare.** Octopus provide ongoing support and aftercare. You can opt for the Octopus Cosy Tariff, which offers cheaper rates at set times. It's still best to check all available tariffs to be sure you find the best tariff for you.

If your house or project are not deemed suitable for an Octopus installation they should offer to pass your details to a vetted local installer. We have now been through this process, and I can report it is quite stringent with real checks of the quality of installations. It could be a helpful route if you are struggling to find a credible installer.

Retrofit projects: Initial estimates

Some installers offer a site survey visit immediately to give a more accurate estimate. While I admire the old-school feel of this, I would argue that the three or four hours' extra work have to be covered, with that cost needing to be somehow incorporated into the price of the installation. The more time spent on surveys that don't turn into sales, the higher the company's cost of sale. This is why I argue that the swift sense check of a desktop guide estimate is advantageous for everyone.

An immediate site survey appointment is likely to be offered by a company where the business owner is carrying out the survey themselves. This is for the reason mentioned above: the cost of sales. As an owner manager, you are not a salaried member of staff and might ignore the cost implication, focusing on being paid from the overall company profits. A slightly larger company will be sending an expensive senior member of salaried staff to carry out the survey.

Many companies will start the sales journey by offering you a guide estimate, though other terms may be used, such as *initial estimate* or *indicative quote*. At R A

Brown Heating Services we've recently improved our estimating process by introducing software that allows technical sales staff to produce a guide estimate during the initial conversation. The advantage of this is it quickly removes ambiguity from the discussion.

I have produced a video, together with our technical sales lead, talking through the information contained in a guide estimate provided by the platform we use, Spruce, which is growing in popularity with installers.[44] You can see how it is possible to improve the accuracy of the guide estimate if you have more information on your floor structure, windows, insulation, etc.

Most software used by installers will base estimates on an up-to-date EPC. This isn't perfect because it doesn't provide as much information about your property as the heat loss survey, but it is an excellent place to start. It can provide a rough indication of the size of heat pump required and from that some initial costings.

If you don't have a realistic idea of budget, when you receive your guide estimate your journey may end very quickly or take a different route such as going with Fornax Energy. If you are approaching independent installers or Heat Geek as an alternative to a utility installer, be prepared – the price might be higher. If you're following the installer search method I gave in

Chapter Five, you may want to approach three or four different installers and compare how they respond to your inquiry.

If you are getting estimates way ahead of the time you need the new heat pump system, that is fine – companies that work on self-build and renovation projects are really used to incredibly long lead-conversion times. We have projects that take over two years to come to fruition. Obviously, prices will change over that time!

HOT TIP: CREATING YOUR OWN ESTIMATE

Trawling the internet, putting your EPC details into different providers' online calculators, can be confusing.

Instead, I recommend you use Nesta's Cost Estimator.[45] This is a piece of software that bases an estimate on your EPC, with that estimate coming from a neutral source rather than from a company wanting to sell their services.

When to get a new EPC

Remember that with a large project, such as adding an extension or significantly upgrading your property, your current EPC won't be accurate. The guide estimate will need to be based on what your property will be like once the project is finished. You will need to provide your plans, and the estimate will take longer and won't be able to be produced instantly over the phone.

HOT TIPS: EPC-READY

For a retrofit: If you have no up-to-date EPC, it's helpful to get one so you can get guide estimates.

Often an installer might be able to recommend an EPC assessor.

Avoid cheap desk-based EPCs, as they are often not accurate.

Things to look for and questions to ask in the conversation about the guide estimate

Talking through the guide estimate offers an excellent opportunity to begin to get to know how your potential installer works.

1. A product suggestion on the guide estimate is a good way to start the discussion. Ask the installer about the makes of heat pump they install and why.

   A serious heat pump installer will usually offer more than one make of product. You are looking for answers, including that they have an existing relationship with the manufacturer, that they are experienced with the product, and that they've completed training with this manufacturer.

2. If you are planning extensive work to your property, ask the installer what services they offer and how they tie in with other contractors.
3. Ask what the next steps are, to get an idea of their process and who is involved, for example how big their team is and who you will be dealing with on the journey.

HOT TIP: PEACE OF MIND

An experienced, knowledgeable installer can install many types of heat pump, but they won't be able to offer extended warranties on all of them.

I recommend choosing an installer who offers an extended product warranty.

Getting the most out of the survey visit

Whether it's the first or second step, a site survey visit is essential because the installer is expected to design the heat pump system fully. If you have a house with over 150 square metres of floor area, you can expect the survey to take more than two hours.

The person doing the survey will need to collect enough data about your house to produce a heat loss survey report. This involves measuring every room and every window, and looking at the construction of the house – the type of glazing, the insulation, the floor, the roof, etc. Some of this is covered on an EPC but not in the detail required.

There are some high-tech bits of survey kit around these days, including LiDar (light detection and ranging) scanning technology, where the surveyor positions a tripod in each room and the equipment scans and measures. Heat Geeks have an iPad with a similar function. This type of scan might look fancier, but a person with a tape measure or laser measure is fine too.

The survey should cover:

- Electricity supply assessment
- Heat loss survey report data collection
- Survey of current radiators and pipework
- Identification of potential outdoor unit positions and noise assessment data collection
- Identification of position for indoor unit, hot water cylinder and controller
- An initial discussion about how the system will be controlled, including the change from thermostatic controls

Inside the house

It is important to provide information about your existing electricity supply. It is usual to include a photo of your main fuseboard (also known as a distribution board or consumer unit), and you will need to provide information about any available 'spurs' or circuits. Any need to upgrade your electricity needs to be ascertained as soon as possible. See the link to the article about electrical supply information in the Recommended Further Reading section at the end of this book.[46]

The surveyor will need to assess your existing heat emitters (radiators or underfloor heating) and look at the size of the pipework. Pipes start larger and become narrower as they run through the property. The initial flow and return pipes should be at least 28 mm, reducing down to 22 mm, and then the usual pipe size running to the radiators is 15 mm. If you have microbore pipework (10 mm or 8 mm), this can be more challenging for the system design. The surveyor will measure and note the types of the radiators.

If you have carried out the *What if... e*xercise in Chapter Four, you can discuss your findings with the surveyor. You can also provide information about how you use your heating system currently and ask about how they approach design, including flow temperatures and their stance on radiator upgrades. Do they design at a high temperature with few radiator upgrades or at low temperature with significant radiator changes?

Outside the house

You may already have a position in mind for your outdoor unit. Don't forget that pipes have to run back to the hot water cylinder from the outdoor unit. Talk this over with the surveyor. Ask about the height of the unit, particularly if it is to be installed underneath a window. The unit cannot be installed as close to the house wall as you might expect – it needs a specific clearance space at both the front and back, with that space depending on the make of heat pump. Ask the surveyor to show you the measurements.

The flow and return pipes are usually neatly installed in flat trunking, and you can often choose between black or white for this.

It is not ideal to install the unit in a shady corridor down the side of your house. The efficiency of the unit can be reduced by the expelled cold air being drawn back into the unit. The installer should be able to advise you of the optimal position.

The surveyor needs to measure the distance that the unit will be positioned from any neighbours' openable windows, to carry out the noise assessment to meet MCS regulations.

Permitted development rules

In most situations an ASHP can be installed without planning permission, as long as it meets permitted development criteria, which were relaxed in spring 2025.

At the time of writing, permitted development rules are:

- Heat pumps can be installed within 1 metre of the property boundary if they pass the noise assessment criteria (MCS 020 standard).
- The size limit of the heat pump for dwelling houses is now 1.5 square metres.
- Two heat pump units are now permitted for detached dwelling houses.
- Air-to-air heat pumps that can provide both heating and cooling are to be included in MCS guidelines and will be eligible for a BUS grant of £2,500.

If you live in a conservation area, the above rules on permitted development may not apply, and it is advisable to seek advice on planning permission.

Heat pump sizing

Two of the questions I hear the most are:

- Why do all the quotes recommend different-sized heat pump units?
- What do I need to heat my house effectively?

I'm going to cover the reasons for different heat loss outcomes in the next chapter, eg why one survey calculates your heat loss to be 6.77 kW, another 7.20 kW and another 8.00 kW. In this section I'll explore the reasons that different companies will specify products with different kilowatt ratings in their quotes.

The installer is expected to provide a minimum temperature of 21°C in your main living areas when it is freezing outside. Different areas of the country have varying *design temperatures* of around -2°C and -5°C. A design temperature is a specified temperature that the designer must use – the system must be capable of providing 21°C of heat in the property when the outside temperature falls to the specified design temperature. This means the system is meeting 100% of the heat loss at the specified design temperature. In our example report the calculated heat loss was 6.77 kW.[47] The installer will look at the technical data for the heat pump brands that they prefer to install and will find a unit that can provide at least 6.77 kW at the outside design temperature. It is important to remember that units are not available in every kilowatt increment.

HOT TIP: CHECK THE 'BADGED' OUTPUT

The 'badged' heat pump output kilowatt rating of a unit usually relates to its output at 7°C outdoor temperature and is therefore misleading.[48]

Ask the installer what the output of the proposed unit is at the outdoor design temperature. It is this figure that you would expect to be reasonably close to your calculated heat loss figure.

Comparison of badged output and actual output at design temperature

Here is a real example of the data of a unit, comparing badged output and actual output at a design temperature of -5°C, which is one of the required design temperatures in Scotland.

At a design temp of -5°C outside, with a 45°C flow temperature, a high-quality heat pump brand running on R290 refrigerant would achieve the following output levels:

- 16 kW badged unit delivers 8.29 kW of heat
- 12 kW badged unit delivers 7.52 kW of heat
- 10 kW badged unit delivers 7.49 kW of heat

You can see there are just 800 kilowatts' difference in output between the 16 kW unit and the 10 kW unit. It is likely that all three units have the same compressor. Now you can see what your installer is up against in terms of specifying the correct unit for your property.

The above illustration shows the difference in output from just one make and model, and you will be looking at proposals of several different makes and models. It would be beneficial if all of the different designers and specifiers didn't come up with different kilowatt options. The most straightforward thing to focus on as a homeowner is checking with the installer what they have calculated your heat requirement to be in kW and then asking them for the output figure at the specified MCS design temperature. This output figure should be larger than the heat loss figure. Remember they must cover the heat loss at the specified design temperature. Even if this seems a bit technical, ask your potential installer.

Hopefully the above example also takes away some of your fear about oversizing. Also, most modern heat pumps modulate – when they don't need to work at full capacity, they adjust themselves down. As a rule of thumb, it is acceptable to see oversizing of around 10% above the calculated heat loss.

Many utility and national installers offer very limited ranges of heat pumps. This isn't a big concern as long as they have a unit that adequately covers your heat loss. This could be one of the reasons, if you have a bigger, older house, that national installers might say they can't provide an installation and suggest you make contact with one of their trusted (accredited) partners. Some small installers may be partnered with a single manufacturer – that's fine too.

What about sizing for a low heat loss house?

If you are building a highly insulated small property, you may come up against the dilemma of needing to focus more on hot water demand than on heating. Your heat loss could be very low, for example 3 kW, which is just the power of a kettle.

There are two factors to consider here:

- You are unlikely to get a heat pump of only 3 kW, with many manufacturers' ranges starting at 5 or 6 kW.
- You are likely to want your hot water to be reheated within a reasonable length of time – no more than 120 minutes. Imagine using the power in a kettle to heat 150 litres of water even to 55°C – it would take a long time!

For a property with this type of very low heat demand, expect the installer to focus on the hot water more than the heating, although all the calculations will be based on the same factors – keeping you warm when it's cold outside, and keeping your supply of hot water flowing.

HOT TIP: BEING OVERSIZED ISN'T A PROBLEM

Don't get hung up about a seemingly oversized heat pump for a highly insulated house with low heat demand – 5 or 6 kW is fine.

What about the sizing if you need multiple heat pumps?

At the other end of the spectrum, if you are installing a heat pump on a large, older property you may be faced with the situation of not being able to find a sufficiently large unit.

There are sometimes advantages to having two units installed in a cascade arrangement, and specialist, experienced installers will be familiar with designing this kind of system. If your heating requirement is, for example, over 14 kW, the installer may recommend a cascade system with multiple units of differing kilowatt ratings.

One advantage of multiple heat pumps is that the electricity required for starting up is reduced as the units won't usually come on at the same time. This can mean you are able to change to a heat pump without upgrading your electricity supply to a three-phase supply (which can be expensive). Three-phase supply is an upgrade to the amount of electricity available. A standard domestic single-phase supply provides

230 volts, and an upgraded three-phase supply provides 400 volts. This is only required for very large properties or commercial premises – your installer should advise you.

Cascade systems are also often very efficient to run, as for much of the year one heat pump provides heating and hot water, while the other unit contributes only during colder weather.

If you live in an especially large property, it is perfectly feasible to install multiple heat pump systems cascading up to nine units. Any more than that, and you need to move to commercial-size units, for which you will need planning permission and sufficient electricity supply.

Warm wisdom – key points

- **Initial process.** The typical process from initial inquiry to contract preparation involves five steps, with some variations in the first two steps for retrofit heat pumps and new-build, renovation and extension projects. There will be variations in those steps with different types of installers.
- **Initial estimates.** Some installers offer a site survey visit at the start of the sales process, though that is likely to increase overall costs.

Other companies, including my own, start with a guide estimate based on an up-to-date EPC.

- **Initial discussions.** When you have received your estimate, it's best to talk this over with your potential installer, asking them about makes of heat pumps, the services they offer, the next steps in the process and extended warranties.
- **Site survey report.** This report, based on thorough internal and external assessment, should cover electricity supply assessment, heat loss survey report data, survey of current radiators and pipework, identification of positions for the outdoor unit, indoor unit and hot water cylinder. Noise assessment data and how the system will be controlled should also be included.
- **Heat pump sizing.** Different companies will specify products with different kilowatt ratings, their main aim being to provide a 21°C temperature in your main living areas when it is freezing outside. Varying sizes and numbers of heat pumps cater for everything from tiny houses to much larger properties.

SEVEN
Final Contract Stages

The final contract stages are of course crucial in ensuring you have chosen the best installer for your needs and that all the points in the proposal are watertight. In this chapter I will outline the final process before you sign the contract, helping you towards peace of mind and confidence that every aspect of your new heat pump installation is suitable for your needs.

Understanding and discussing the proposal

The proposal or quote document produced following the heat loss survey visit is likely to be a long and quite complex report. You can become familiar with all of the areas it covers by looking at the example I've provided in the Resources area of our website: https://rabrown.co.uk/sample-heat-loss-report. I'm going to walk you through it now.

Information on the heat loss calculations

- The calculated figure for the heat loss of your property should be prominent on the report. It will be a figure displayed in kilowatts, eg 6.77 kW.
- For you to be warm, your heating system needs to deliver heat to your radiators or UFH as quickly as the house is losing it.
- The quote should clearly show the outdoor design temperature (-3.1°C) used and a figure showing heating degree days. These will help you with your detective work in comparing reports from different installers.
- The clearly laid out information, such as that provided by design software, can help you see for yourself the basis for the installer's recommendations of certain products or radiator upgrades.
- Many reports will show the heat loss calculated for each room and provide information on the criteria the surveyor used, for example, the choices they made on the thermal values of your house.

- Air changes per hour (ACH) of each room are taken into consideration. Different areas of your house might be judged to have more or fewer air changes per hour, and if different surveyors make different decisions on this, the overall heat loss figure produced will be different. As a lay person, it is possible to discuss air changes – think of it like this: a draughty room has significantly more air changes. This can be caused by ill-fitting doors or windows or an open chimney. A centrally situated room with no draughts is an area you would expect the installer to reduce the air changes in to create a more accurate heat loss figure.

System design or product information

- You can expect to see a proposal for at least one heat pump and for the full details to be provided, including that it is an MCS registered product.
- The proposal report should include the capacity of the heat pump at a particular flow temperature, for example, 45°C – it also shows the manufacturer's stated SCOP at that flow temperature.
- It is helpful to see the capability of the heat pump to provide sufficient heat for your house at varying outdoor temperatures. Popular platforms such as Spruce show the capability

of the heat pump. This is displayed in a table labelled *Capacity*.

- There is also a table showing the SCOP at different flow temperatures. Hopefully you're beginning to see that heat pump efficiency is a balance between a suitably sized unit, emitters correctly sized to work at a chosen flow temperature, and the fact that variable outdoor temperatures will affect the amount of electricity used.

HOT TIP: FLOW TEMPERATURES

All the information within the proposal or quote document can be useful if you want to discuss opting for a higher or lower flow temperature. Remember that high flow temperature can mean fewer radiator changes are needed but incur higher running costs.

You can expect to see a list of proposed radiator changes, with a traffic light system to show that the proposed radiator can supply sufficient heat for the room.

Hot water

In the design you should see a specific cylinder with size in litres, for example, 200 litres and a proposed location. With a Spruce report there is a whole page detailing the calculations for hot water demand, energy required and safety measures such as the legionella cycles. It is important for lower water temperature systems that the temperature is raised sufficiently to kill bacteria such as legionella.

MCS 031 performance estimate

This section is a mandatory part of the report that compares fossil fuel options such as mains gas with a heat pump in terms of running costs and carbon savings. MCS want installers to show the potential performance of the designed system at a standardised seasonal performance factor (SPF), which is set at 3.4 – or 340% efficiency – for heating. The idea is that if all system designs are displayed using the same SPF, it removes the possibility that manufacturers are making exaggerated claims about their products' performance.

Note: *SPF* and *SCOP* are commonly used interchangeably.

HOT TIP: COMPARING REPORTS

You can use the MCS 031 performance estimate page to make a direct comparison and spot the differences between the calculations of the different surveyors, and thereby the strengths of the different products.

That's pretty much where MCS 031's usefulness starts and ends. MCS 031 is of very limited use for the homeowner as it standardises the estimated output across all systems being designed. The MCS standard is designed to prevent installers from over-claiming on the efficiency of the system, but, in reality, it has the opposite effect by 'dumbing down' the figures and making accurate decision-making harder for the consumer. Installers of quality systems want to show you the potentially much better performance of the products they are offering, including a table that shows the manufacturers' efficiency ratings. You will see the efficiency of hot water separated, because heating is more energy-efficient than hot water. The hot water is therefore usually heated to a higher temperature – for example, if the heating is designed to have a flow temperature of 45°C, the hot water needs to be heated to at least 55°C.

The performance efficiency results table shows estimated energy consumption based on manufacturers' test data, and it compares energy usage with your current fuel, eg mains gas. Finally, it estimates the kilogrammes of carbon saved per year – a satisfying figure to look at if your motivation is to reduce your carbon footprint.

HOT TIP: ENERGY CONSUMPTION MONITORING

In the MCS 031 you will find an energy consumption figure that is also used to calculate an electricity usage and price estimate.

It's satisfying to see energy use for heating and hot water reduced, with a heat pump typically providing a 75% reduction when compared with mains gas. An efficient heat pump system should use 25% of fuel when compared.

System efficiency

This section of the proposal or quote document, as presented by Spruce software, summarises much of the same data again, but there is one interesting figure to highlight: that of hot water efficiency. In addition to requiring a heating performance of 3.4, the MCS 031 specify a requirement for the hot water efficiency to be 1.7, or 170%, which is very low. We put the manufacturer data next to the standardised estimate levels; on the product in my example quote the hot water SCOP is 3.35. I'm not convinced these MCS 031 figures help you make a decision. Manufacturer data might not be perfect, but I think for quality brands it is likely to be more accurate than these poor, dumbed-down, standardised figures.

Pricing

In addition to the information about your house (heat loss), system design and products, the proposal or quote will include the price. The cost breakdown should:

- Be broken down into sections, including the cost of the heat pump and associated equipment, with the cylinder price shown separately or included in the cost of a bundle of equipment

- Usually include the cost of radiator upgrades, with a labour price for all the work; sometimes labour is itemised for different parts of the work, or it can be shown as a total labour figure for the whole job
- Possibly, depending on the installer, include an estimate or quote for electrical work
- Usually quote for all the work, the total shown at the end with the BUS grant deducted
- Include a list of exclusions, which will help you compare what different installers are providing

How to make the final decisions on your new system

There is of course a lot more to buying a heat pump than replacing a boiler. It is the first time your house will have been surveyed in this way and the first time you'll have had a low water temperature system designed. It's an exciting transition but one that requires careful absorption of information. In fact, all retrofit heating systems would benefit if they were always calculated and specified in this way.

HOT TIP: CRITICAL EVALUATION

Sit down with all the information you have gathered from estimates, quotes, conversations and self-assessments of your house.

Ask yourself the following questions:

- Which one of the installers stood out? Which one provided the clearest information, answered questions well and presented the survey and quote comprehensively?
- Are you confident about the details of what's being offered? If not, what else do you need to find out?
- Do you feel confident to pick the best installer for your project?
- Do you know which product you want to have installed – the make, model, warranty, kilowattage?
- What flow temperature appeals – 35/45/55°C – and how many new radiators are needed for each option?
- Are you comfortable about the quoted price? Can you afford it outright, or how else will you finance the system?
- Do you know exactly what is included and what you have to arrange (such as a concrete pad or paving slab base for the heat pump to sit on, or a skip to dispose of waste)?
- Have you been given full information about where the disruption will be, for example in the removal of the old pipes and cylinder (or a discussion about the possibility of retaining your current cylinder), installation of pipes from the heat pump and into the house?

- Are you happy with the position and size of the hot water cylinder? Have you measured up and visualised how it will fit?
- Do you know where the outdoor unit is going to be sited, how big it is, the clearances it needs around it and how the pipes will run from it? Will the pipes be only lagged or also hidden in ducting?
- What components are being fitted into the boiler cupboard or plant room?

Schedule an in-depth run-through with the installer

Either before or after signing the contract, it is a good idea to ask the installer to run through the technical details thoroughly. It might be that the specifier, designer or salesperson needs to hand the project over to the senior engineer and that you can join in with their own run-through.

This is an opportunity for you to clarify a number of points, including:

- What components are being fitted into the boiler cupboard or plant room
- Whether your system is designed to work with a buffer vessel or volumiser
- What the controller looks like and where it will be situated

- How the system will be controlled, and what zones or areas there will be – you want to ascertain what you can turn off or down, such as TRVs on bedroom radiators
- What the pipe spacing will be if you are having underfloor heating
- Whether photos will be provided of the layout for future reference (if you want a full, detailed schematic plan, there may be an additional fee)

If your project is a new-build, renovation or extension, it is crucial also to ask the heating installer if the architect has allowed adequate space for the plant room. We work with many wonderful architects, but some have no idea of the space needed and only allow an inadequately sized cupboard. This can end up costing you more as equipment then has to be sited more remotely – often in a garage – and running the low loss pipe, for example across a courtyard, is expensive and creates additional work.

Timing

It's important when discussing the proposal to focus on whether you need a new system as quickly as possible or are planning a little way ahead. It is perfectly acceptable to go on the journey of discovery and then decide your boiler might last a little while longer. If you feel you've formed a positive rapport with an installer but want to postpone the start of the project, simply take the time to explain that to the installer, committing to going back to them when you're ready.

HOT TIP: IN CASE OF A DELAY TO THE PROJECT

Keep records of all that you've learned and give a clear indication about when you'd like to talk again.

Remember that the work will likely need to be repriced and that the contract will need to be signed and a deposit paid before the work can be booked in.

Smart controls

Many people who are thinking of switching to heat pumps are also interested in smart, app-based tech, which is understandable if you want to see how the new heating system is performing. In this section I'll signpost you to platforms and apps to explore smart controls further.

HOT TIPS: APP CHOICES

- It is best to avoid smart apps that control thermostats. These are intended to make boiler systems 'smarter', but many heat pumps have sophisticated controls built in. You should ensure that these controls are fully set up before the system is handed over to you, rather than buying a third-party app without consultation.
- You need to check if the heat pump you're buying offers remote monitoring and

connectivity accessible for both you and your installer. Can you alter the system settings remotely before you get home from your holiday?

- Some people do add additional specialist monitoring packages such as those offered by Open Energy Monitor (see below). They can be expensive, however.

Here are some smart control software platforms I'm familiar with:

- **Adia.** This is quite new but has already won an innovation award. Its aim is to balance comfort and cost savings, with the system monitoring how your system is performing. It is connected to the heat pump, collecting live data about the water temperature, which is displayed in an app, and also links to smart electricity tariffs. We haven't tried it yet, and currently not all makes of heat pump are compatible, but some of our industry contacts are finding promising results.[49]
- **Havenwise.** This software, designed specifically to work with heat pumps, is gaining popularity and is compatible with a range of makes of heat pump. With the aim of reducing bills by optimising the system, it is attractive to both homeowners and installers. If your heat pump doesn't come with suitable software, this might be worth considering.[50]

- **Homely.** This is an app-based monitoring system, reportedly working with most heat pumps, so is useful for makes that don't have their own apps. It works with electricity tariffs, claiming to save money on your bills.[51]
- **Open Energy Monitor.** This is 'heavyweight' monitoring tech that costs several hundred pounds without installation. The creators have a very good reputation in the industry, and quite a few of the top heat pump engineers monitor their own installs using this. We haven't used it as we generally rely on the manufacturer's monitoring software.[52]
- **Hive Home.** Hive, a well-known brand name in smart thermostats, are owned by Centrica and as such are moving into the space of air source heat pump installation as well as solar PV, battery, EV chargers, etc. They are currently partnered with British Gas and seem to have plans to expand their installer network soon.[53]

  On how their smart controls work with heat pumps (weather compensation continues, if enabled within the heat pump), Hive explains that there are two ways Hive can connect:

  - **Via a fitted Hive thermostat:** The weather compensation will still run as long as the manufacturer allows this in their unit when an external thermostat is fitted. The weather compensation continues to be performed by the heat pump controller, not by the Hive thermostat.

- **Via cloud-to-cloud connection with no additional hardware:** Hive doesn't touch the weather compensation settings, meaning it will continue to be performed by the heat pump controller as normal.[54]

Hive's integration with heat pumps at this stage is therefore about connectivity to the Hive ecosystem (and by extension tariffs and other household devices) and monitoring / data / diagnostics.

Note: The same advice applies to all brands of smart thermostats – they are unlikely to work well with a heat pump as you want to use weather compensation, not thermostatic control.

There are other very inexpensive ways of monitoring how much power your heat pump is using. Look at the submeter on the electricity supply to the heat pump system, or at the controller's record of electricity consumed by the heat pump itself. If neither of these works for you, it is straightforward to buy monitors online.

HOT TIP: ASK YOUR INSTALLER TO SET UP WEATHER COMPENSATION

Your installer may have a lot of information to share about the best way to control your system, or they may be clueless. Either way, a word of warning: don't ask your installer to set your system to run off a 'traditional' third-party thermostat control app. Heat pump installers owe it to the customer to assertively advise against this, but not all installers work with that kind of confidence.

I recommend talking this through rather than asking your installer to connect things up in a particular way. I have heard many stories of homeowners declining the weather compensation function being turned on when their system is set up, only to regret that omission later.

Warm wisdom – key points

- **Reviewing the proposal.** Allow yourself some quiet time to go through the proposal report, noting questions or anything you want clarification on, including heat loss calculations, system design, product information and system efficiency.
- **Pricing.** The proposal should have a clear breakdown of costs, including the cost of the heat pump and associated equipment radiator upgrades, labour costs and a list of exclusions, which will help you compare what different installers are providing.
- **Evaluation.** It's important you compare the documents and information you have from all installers, as well as your general experience with them to date. Refer to the 'Hot tip:

Critical evaluation' in this chapter for a full list of things to consider. After that, ask for an in-depth run-through with the installer to gain clarification on any outstanding questions.

- **Smart controls.** I recommend avoiding third-party apps where possible, if the manufacturer's own app is user-friendly and reliable. Having said that, there are exciting innovations, such as Adia, gaining popularity among experienced installers. Ensure you ask your installer to activate weather compensation before final signoff, as this will allow you to improve efficiency and comfort when using your new heat pump.

PART FOUR

INSTALLATION AND OTHER TECHNOLOGIES

EIGHT

Installation And Living With A Heat Pump

In this chapter I will help you through the remaining stages of acquiring a heat pump, including contract signoff and project handover. I'll also give you an idea of the disruption you will encounter during installation and how long that disruption will last, before helping you see how different your life will be once you have your new heat pump installed.

The contract, installation and handover

Because you are buying a heat pump via an MCS registered installer, you will find MCS related mandatory documents together with your contract. There will also be additional mandatory paperwork if you are claiming the BUS grant. While there is a lot of paperwork, it is worth reading it carefully.

HOT TIP: BUS GRANT REMINDER

The BUS grant should appear as a figure deducted from the total of your quote.

The installer is required to apply for and redeem a voucher after completion.

Before the proposal is turned into a contractual document, take time to sort all the finer details, including, for example, the exact radiators you want. If details are altered later, variation contracts will be needed.

The contract pack will vary from installer to installer, but they should always include:

- A link to 'Guidance for Property Owners' produced by Ofgem (the energy regulator for Great Britain) about the BUS grant.[55] This is an installer led process, but you need to provide the required information for the application.
- Details of all the products being supplied and the cost of labour, which should be included in the proposal document itself. There should be a detailed exclusions list too.
- The installation company's own code of practice or terms of business. These will be individual, not stipulated by MCS, so are worth reading carefully.

- A payment schedule showing a breakdown of payments, with the BUS grant shown separately. It is usual to pay a 25% deposit to secure your space in the installer's diary and a second instalment to cover the heat pump and cylinder being ordered. Some companies don't take a deposit, but most can't afford to work without this security.
- A notice of your right to cancel the contract within fourteen days and the terms for this. This is a mandatory MCS document.
- A contract of sale, signed away from the installer's premises. This is a mandatory MCS document but can be customised to some extent by each company.
- An ENA (Energy Networks Association) notification to confirm that you will notify the Distribution Network Operator (DNO). This will be included somewhere in the contract, and your installer will submit the ENA on your behalf. You will need to confirm the MPAN (meter point administration number, shown on your electricity bill) and site address. See Electrical Supply Information link in the Resources section on our website: https://rabrown.co.uk/category/resources.
- A customer warranty document giving you information about consumer protection bodies RECC (Renewable Energy Consumer Code) and

HIES. These may be replaced in 2026 by MCS's own Customer Commitment document.[56]

- An express consent form, if you need the work to start within the fourteen-day cooling-off period. You can sign this express consent form to waive the cooling-off period.

If any of these items are missing from your contract pack, question that with your installer.

HOT TIPS: FINAL CHECKS

Check the exclusions list carefully as items not included may need you to do something. An exclusions list might include installation of sanitary ware and showers, creation of a base for ASHP and removal of tanks in the roof.

Utility companies such as Octopus have items such as pipework replacement in their exclusions list. They test for asbestos and expect you to get it removed if any is found.

How much disruption you can expect during an installation

There is variation in the time required for installation and the disruption involved. It can be much less stressful if you know what is going to happen, so this section is designed to give you some insight and peace of mind.

You should start by asking your installer how long the installation will take for a retrofit project. It is likely to be between three and ten days. For a new build, the timescales are linked to the build. The installer will work with your project manager and the project manager will keep the heating company informed on progress.

HOT TIP: SECURE A DATE

As soon as you've paid the deposit, get your job booked into the installer's diary for a time that suits you.

Several factors can affect the total installation time and level of disruption:

- The fewer radiator changes you need, the less disruption you're likely to have.
- If you make sure there is access to where the outside unit will be installed and to the cylinder cupboard so that the installers can get on with their work quickly and easily.
- The installers will start by removing the old boiler and cylinder, so you need to check on the arrangements for having the gas supply capped off.
- The price of the work will usually include removal of the old equipment, but if this is in the

exclusions list, you will need to dispose of old radiators and pieces of pipes, etc.

- It is essential for pipes to come through walls. All pipework should be neatly lagged with specific insulation that includes weather proofing (UV protection).
- Find out if re-piping of radiators is needed and if flooring needs to be lifted.
- Find out how long you will be without heating and hot water so you can make arrangements to reduce your stress and discomfort.
- Ask the installation team where they will be working and which rooms will be disruption free so that you know what areas you will need to avoid.
- Ask when the electrician will be onsite and how much time the power will be turned off for.

Initial handover and learning how your system works

The handover happens in two stages:

1. A physical run through with the chief engineer after commissioning
2. A physical or digital handover pack of documentation

HOT TIP: RECORD THE INSTALLER HANDOVER

A video or a voice recorder with transcription works well so you have a record you can refer to afterwards, including the answers to questions you ask.

What to expect in the handover pack

The main documents that should be included at handover include:

- A summary document with installer details, system details and handover information, as well as advice on how to access follow-up support
- A warranty information sheet – there is a generic workmanship warranty of two years and product warranties, and the installer should register the products with the manufacturer(s)
- Maintenance log and service schedule (manufacturer's documents)
- Commissioning check sheets applicable to your installation
- Product handbooks in paper form or information with links to digital versions
- MCS installation registration certificate, with the installer having registered the installation

Aftersales and living with your new system

Congratulations – you're now ready to begin your cosy new journey. Here are a few things you can expect soon:

- If your installation takes place in the heating season, many installers will routinely book in a follow-up visit to check you're comfortable and to tweak settings if needed.
- By now you should have a good relationship with your installer. Do check anything you're not sure about, by email if they are 'on the tools', unless your query is urgent.
- If there is someone with a deep technical interest in your household, they may have already decided on extra monitoring apps, as discussed in Chapter Seven. It's usually possible to get into monitoring later on if you want to.
- You should try to be bold with allowing your house to run as an open loop and letting the weather compensation achieve the nice, even warmth.
- If you're too hot, it is often possible to adjust the heat curves with some over-the-phone guidance.
- It may take a little while to get the settings spot on. Don't fiddle with the controls too much

– you'll know it's right when you've forgotten about it.

Note: When you've settled in with your system, you could sign your house up to Nesta's Visit a Heat Pump scheme to allow other people to gain inspiration and feedback from you.

HOT TIP: FEEDBACK

Provide feedback to your installer.

If the experience was good, give them a review on whatever platforms they use such as Google.

Annual servicing

Here are some pointers on what you need to know about annual servicing:

- To maintain your product warranty, it is important to have your system serviced annually.
- Ideally use the company that installed your heat pump, as they will know the system better than anyone else. If this isn't possible, contact the manufacturer for alternative servicing options.
- If you have opted for a Fornax Energy monthly package, servicing is included.

- The annual servicing visit should last for about an hour and be comprehensive, including:
  - The covers being taken off the outside unit, and inspecting and cleaning of the heat pump components
  - Checks of how many times the compressor has started in the year and other heat pump settings being checked at the controller
  - Checks of the vessels in the plant room or boiler cupboard

Running costs

Costs are dependent on electricity prices and the efficiency of the system, but running a heat pump will for most people be cheaper than using a fossil fuel system. There should be no nasty surprises relating to system efficiency. If you've had a Heat Geek ZeroDisrupt installation, you should have a guaranteed minimum performance. Do speak with the installation company and MCS if you're not sure the system is meeting expected running costs and levels of efficiency.

HOT TIP: REDUCING ENERGY COSTS

Look out for the best time-of-use tariffs or off-peak tariffs and switch when needed.

CASE STUDY: Paul Eastwood's Lived Experience

Paul Eastwood is a homeowner and sustainability professional, living in Glasgow, who has documented his experience of buying a heat pump in LinkedIn blogs. Paul's property is a Victorian terrace house. He has kindly agreed with us sharing the following case study describing his lived experience.

Paul's advice: Your house probably is suitable for a heat pump

I still keep seeing articles about heat pumps not being suitable for UK homes. Well, the new air source heat pump installed in my home over the summer seems to be working just fine. It had its first real test recently, when it reached 3°C overnight. The inside temperature never dropped below 17.5°C and comfortably maintained 18.5–19°C average temperature throughout the day, and did so using less than a quarter of the energy than a typical winter's day last year when we heated our home with gas.

Since last winter we have increased the level of insulation in the roof and installed triple glazing in some of the windows (the remainder are double glazed), so those measures should be helping. Otherwise, it is a typical British mid-terrace, built 120 years ago when insulation and airtightness were not design considerations. Floors and external walls are uninsulated.

Somewhat counterintuitively, it feels warmer inside even though the radiators are generally cooler to the touch. Because the system is running all of the time, the set temperature levels inside the house are maintained more evenly. The water flowing through the radiators ranges between 20°C and 35°C, depending on outside temperatures. It will be interesting to see how the system performs at subzero temperatures, but so far my experience is of a warmer home using far less energy, with no direct carbon emissions.

How to run your heat pump system

In another post Paul shared what he's learned from living with a heat pump, answering a question: 'Running your heat pump all day doesn't sound very energy-efficient?'

Paul's answer:

A high water temperature of, say, 70°C will very quickly increase the indoor temperature when it's relatively warm outside, but not in an energy-efficient way. An outdoor thermostat tells the heat pump how much to heat the water by to replace the loss of heat from the building. Typically, the water in our heating circuit doesn't rise above 40°C (it hasn't fallen below zero outside for more than brief periods yet) but can be as low as 20°C. For this reason we use a setback of 18°C at night and during the day while we are at work.

We would turn our gas boiler off when going away in winter, and it would take a full day to raise the temperature from single digits to the high teens because of our thick stonework. A heat pump could do the same by setting a high water temp but would cost more in electricity and not be efficient. A more efficient approach is to go slowly and steadily, using a lower heating temperature of 35–45°C, which reduces the consumption of electricity but takes longer to raise the indoor temperature.

Learning about heat curves

In another post Paul shared what he's learned about controlling the heat curves on his system:

It's taken me a while to make sense of how a heat pump is controlled as there is no indoor thermostat. That was the biggest surprise when my heat pump was installed – how do I set the indoor temperature when the heat pump only knows what the outside temperature is? When it is 0°C outside (as it is today in Glasgow) and I want 20°C inside, a heating curve of 1 will deliver water at 40°C. If I increase the curve to 1.5, the water temperature will increase to 50°C. Shifting the indoor temperature up or down a degree or two creates a parallel shift in the heating curve, but the slope remains broadly the same. To maximise efficiency, the heating curve should be as low as possible, but set it too low and the water in the heating won't be hot enough to reach the indoor target temperature. For a heat pump to operate at maximum efficiency (and therefore at least cost) a heating curve needs to be found that delivers *just enough* heat – the Micawber Principle of heating.[57]

Warm wisdom takeaways

- Don't accept a verdict that your house isn't suitable for a heat pump or needs a hybrid. Find information on hybrid systems on the Energy Saving Trust website.[58]
- Improving insulation and glazing is beneficial.
- The slow-and-steady approach keeps your house warmer.
- You'll get used to not having a thermostat and tweaking your heat curves.

I heard this story from an episode of Nathan Gambling's *BetaTalk* podcast, in which he interviewed Paul.[59] Have a listen if you want more detailed information.

Warm wisdom – key points

- **The contract pack.** Together with your contract, you should receive a number of other documents from Ofgem, the product manufacturer and MCS, as well as the installer's own papers, own warranties, their code of practice, an express consent form and payment conditions.
- **Disruption during installation.** As with any home improvement project, a certain level of disruption is inevitable. There are various ways it can be lessened in your new project, and communication with your installer on dates and preparation will help to reduce any stress you experience.
- **Living with your new system.** At the start of your cosy new journey, you should expect a routine follow-up visit from the installer, and you need to be able to contact them with any questions while you get used to your new heat pump. It's also vital to arrange annual servicing, and you should have clear oversight of and understanding of running costs.

NINE

Other Technologies That Enhance Your Heat Pump Experience

A great thing about heat pumps is that they complement other eco-friendly technologies, and combining solar PV, battery storage and a heat pump can further reduce your energy bills. Beyond that, combining microgeneration and electricity storage gives a sense of energy security, and some of the apps I mentioned earlier can help tie all of the technologies together.

These extra benefits really stood out during conversations with customers who have opted for similar combinations. It's like being part of an exclusive club, but I of course want this experience to become as inclusive as possible. In this closing chapter we'll look at some other technologies you might like to consider to complement your new heating system.

Microgeneration options

Here's an overview of three new opportunities:

1. Battery storage
2. Solar PV
3. Micro-wind

1. Battery storage

We have added 10 kW of battery storage to our system in two stages over the last few years. It is becoming increasingly common to install electrical batteries that can be charged up from solar PV or off-peak cheap electricity. Electricity prices are burdened with taxes, and the price cap set by Ofgem allows them to be higher than anywhere else in Europe. Between 1 January and 31 March 2026, the energy price cap is set at 27.69 pence per kW hour, a rise of 0.2% from 2025. There are predictions that prices may fall in April 2026.

Octopus and other electricity providers have developed sophisticated time-of-use tariffs, where you can buy electricity at significantly reduced rates during off-peak periods. In our household we use an off-peak tariff that provides electricity at a much lower cost between the hours of 00.30 and 05.30. This is when we charge batteries from mid-autumn to mid-spring, when solar PV production is reduced.

HOT TIP: EXPLOITING OFF-PEAK TARIFFS

Add battery storage to your home and shop around for the best off-peak tariff. If you run your system on weather compensation, with no timed restrictions, you can benefit from running your system for part of the night and into the morning using off-peak rate. This off-peak rate coincides with the coldest part of the day. The batteries can also be used to store electricity from the solar panels during the summer, meaning you can then switch off the overnight off-peak rate charging.

All of this will make your running costs satisfyingly – almost embarrassingly – low.

2. Solar PV

Solar PV panels harness the sun's energy and produce electricity to run any electrical appliances, including an air source heat pump, air conditioning units, a hot tub and electric vehicles.

The slight drawback is that when solar PV is producing at its peak, in summer, you will likely only need your ASHP to produce hot water because heating won't be needed. Modern solar PV produces a useful amount of electricity even in relatively dull conditions.

3. Micro-wind

A small proportion of homeowners, with a favourable location and land around their property, will benefit from installing a small wind turbine to generate electricity throughout the year. You'll need to check planning permission rules before installation.

It is satisfying to create cost-free power on a cloudy day, but a small turbine will produce only a few kilowatts of power, so it is difficult to get a decent payback on investment. Our weather patterns seem to be getting stormier and windier, though, and this technology usually produces most energy during the autumn and winter, ideal for when you are running your heat pump.

CASE STUDY: Microgeneration, Storage and Renewable Heating

Some of our most satisfied customers are those that have opted to install multiple technologies. This mirrors my own lived experience. If you are comfortable, enjoy low running costs and are spending your money in a way that is aligned with your values, it is a recipe for contentment. This is a perfect combination of technologies for high comfort and low running costs.

Retrofit of a riverside townhouse

Diana and Alun moved into their four-storey terraced townhouse, built around 1975, about ten years ago. When they bought it, the house was almost unaltered from when it was built, and the couple set about an immediate extensive renovation project. This involved installation of cavity wall insulation, changing single-glazed windows to triple-glazed units, improving insulation in the loft and the garage roof, creating a loft conversion and having a new gas boiler installed. Underfloor heating was installed in the lounge, which is situated on the first floor.

About eight years later the couple embarked on their Green Project. The idea of switching to a heat pump was discussed with their usual plumber, but this was not something he had experience of. They tried to get a quote from Octopus Energy for solar PV and an ASHP. Octopus deemed their south-facing roof unsuitable for PV, which Diana and Alun knew was incorrect, and they did not like the upfront survey fee. They sought out a solar PV and battery quote from a company recommended by a neighbour. When the couple explained they wanted to get rid of gas, the surveyor made some strange suggestions such as an electric boiler! A recommendation to contact R A Brown Heating Services was eventually made, and the project was planned in autumn 2023 and completed in spring 2024.

The Green Project

The following work was undertaken:

- A new garage door installed and wall insulation added to reduce heat loss, because the garage is part of the house
- Solar PV installed by a local contractor
- Battery storage installed in the garage

- Air source heat pump and some radiator upgrades installed by my company

Project management

One of the factors that led to such a successful multitechnology installation was that Diana took on the role of project manager. Another advantage was how well Diana and Alun knew their house, thanks to a previous significant renovation project.

Diana called a key project meeting with the garage door contractor, the solar PV or battery contractor, R A Brown Heating Services and our specialist electrician. The garage was used as a plant room, with all the equipment positions planned out to millimetre accuracy.

Diana and Alun designated routes for pipes and cabling, utilising service conduits and innovative ideas for boxing in, which they did themselves.

The couple were actively involved in problem solving. For example, the heat loss survey report indicated the need for a larger heat emitter in the kitchen, where space was limited. We suggested a kickspace heater, but Diana and Alun opted for a vertical radiator behind the kitchen door as they did not want to hear the noise of the fan within the kickspace heater. The couple knew their priorities on this, having installed triple glazing to create a quiet environment.

They had a query about the specification of one of the new radiators. It seemed to Diana that a slightly taller version was a more standard size and may have been faster to source as the exactly sized 1.5-metre-tall radiator, which took a long time to arrive. She said she would have been happy to have a 1.6-metre version as with a vertical radiator there is often wiggle room on the space available. Perhaps this is a lesson we can all learn from – not to be afraid to have in-depth discussions with the installer and quiz them until you are satisfied the design meets all of your needs.

The outcome

- Diana and Alun were happy with the quality of the design and installation provided by R A Brown Heating Services. A year and a half on, the project is proving a good return on investment.
- Their bills have dropped from £240 per month to just £70, and they enjoy being good to the environment while creating a warm and comfy home.
- They had been concerned about the detrimental effect of gas on interior air quality, which was solved by completely getting rid of gas from the property.
- The property's EPC rating has improved to a high B, and Diana is hopeful it could rise to an A if solar batteries are included in the assessment.
- Their next planned green purchase is a heat pump tumble dryer.

Update from Diana – October 2025

'Since the initial project was completed we have had three more batteries, another inverter and ten more solar panels installed (on the front of the house), and our monthly bill has gone down from £70 to a notional £1 – the house effectively pays us to heat and light it! We have had the heat pump tumble dryer since last November, and we like it a lot.'

Sharing a positive experience

When I interviewed them for this book, Diana and Alun said they were keen to encourage others to install heat pumps and were enthusiastic to sign up for Nesta's Visit a Heat Pump scheme, meaning you may be able to visit them and speak to them in person. We have had many customers over the years who are now enthusiastic to share their journey.

I was very impressed by this transformation of a city property, which now has a magical, Tardis-like quality. The combination of the plant room and garage is inspiring, as is the quality of the work Diana and Alun have done themselves and the innovative and immaculate way they've hidden the cables and pipe runs.

Diana and Alun were thrilled with the news that we won Air Source Project of the Year for their installation at the ACR and Heat Pump Awards 2025. They have a copy of the award certificate!

Warm wisdom takeaways

- It sounds cheesy, but team work really does make the dream work.
- For the best outcome, really engage with contractors. You don't have to be particularly technical to consider all the options and choices for the system.
- Don't underestimate the eco smugness you will feel when you've completed an extensive decarbonisation project.

Additional technology to control ventilation

As you may be aware, there is much discussion on the topic of improving the air tightness and insulation of properties before installing heat pumps. In this section I'll highlight other technologies that might be useful if your plan is to carry out an extensive refurbishment of your house in addition to installing a heat pump.

If you significantly increase the airtightness of your property, you may need to install some kind of mechanical ventilation with heat recovery (MVHR).

How MVHR works

With MVHR two fans are used to continuously extract stale, moist air from a property and replace it with filtered, prewarmed air from outside. It requires ducting to be installed, leading from and back to a central unit. Benefits include:

- A continuous, controlled flow of fresh air into the property
- A reduction in heat being wasted from bathroom steam extraction
- Heat removed from the steamy air being used to preheat the fresh air, reducing heat loss

While it's harder to run the ductwork discreetly in a retrofit project, it can be possible, and it is easier to retrofit in a bungalow.

Other ventilation options for retrofit

There are two less intrusive ventilation options that are easier than MVHR to fit in existing properties: MEV (mechanical extract ventilation) and CME (continuous mechanical ventilation). It may be worthwhile exploring these options if you are planning to make significant improvements to your airtightness and insulation.

HOT TIP: MEV OR CME FOR BUILDING PROJECTS

Check that this technology is being included, asking your architect about this aspect of your designs.

How to find installers

Here are some brief tips on different search methods for the different technologies:

- **Solar PV and batteries.** This is a thriving market due to high electricity prices, so there are many companies. Use similar methods to the heat pump installer search outline in Chapter Five.
- **Micro-wind.** There is no network of local installers as demand is very low, so look for a larger national provider.

- **MVHR.** Many specialist heat pump installers also install MVHR. If you're struggling to find one, reach out to a quality MVHR manufacturer such as Zehnder. They have a network of partner installers across the UK.[60]

HOT TIP: EXPLORE OPTIONS

Don't forget to shop around for the best off-peak electricity tariff, whether or not you intend to install these additional technologies. It will make a difference to your household bills and you will need a smart meter to access these tariffs.

Warm wisdom – key points

- **Eco-friendly technologies.** If finances allow, there are various other options to further enhance a reduction in energy use and costs, including battery storage, solar PV, micro-wind and various types of ventilation technology. Don't forget also to shop around for the best electricity tariff.
- **Controlling ventilation.** MVHR provides controlled ventilation, ensuring a fresh flow of air and reducing moisture in your property. Improved ventilation is important if you have increased the airtightness and insulation of your property, and the benefits often outweigh the initial cost and inconvenience of installation.

Conclusion

Having spent twenty-three years in the heating industry, I am certain that heat pumps are the best solution for enhancing home comfort while eradicating reliance on fossil fuels. It is true that the initial investment can seem high and that many people are unaware of the generous grants and financing available to make the transition affordable. Although there is a growing desire to decarbonise, there remains a gap in knowledge regarding the full benefits of this technology. I hope Warm Wisdom has provided the insight you need to see the true potential of a heat pump for your home.

By now you should be looking at your house and current heating system through a different lens. I have clarified the finance options available at the time this book was released, which will at least give you a firm foundation for when you start your own project. I've also shed light on all the reasons heat pumps are better than using purely nonrenewable energy.

You now have an understanding of the type of heat pump best suited to your property or building project, including the big debates over radiator upgrades. I think *Warm Wisdom* is unique in that it includes advice on how to find a credible installer, already armed with a clear picture of what you want. I hope you feel empowered by the practical insider journey I have outlined, taking you step by step through the process you'll follow in acquiring a wonderful new heating system for your home.

I began this book looking at the history of heat pumps. I want to end on a crystal ball moment, with my vision for the future of heat pumps in the UK. With so many factors affecting the heating industry, it's hard to predict all new developments, but as of early 2026, focus needs to be placed on the following areas:

- Experimentation with low-disruption retrofit systems
- Increased normalisation of heat pumps in all types of building projects
- A gradual increase in the quality of systems being installed in new-build estates

- A shift to reduce electricity prices, at least for heat pump adopters
- More GSHPs being installed in district or commercial developments
- Gradual training and upskilling of heating engineers to competence in heat pump design and installation
- More separate design companies and software to support installers
- New platforms for homeowners to model the changes they want to make to their properties
- Growing awareness of healthy homes, with controlled ventilation, breathability and airtightness

I read an inspirational book recently – *Stellar* – which begins by painting an apocalyptic picture of our world heading for destruction.[61] In the second half the authors share a utopian vision, essentially of the world being run on free energy from the sun and of exponential possibilities being enabled by AI. I am not certain their vision will become reality, but it is something we can aspire to.

Change can come from the edge, outside of the centre of power. Successive governments in the UK have not fully backed heat pump technology. They have sat on the fence and been swayed by the 'old money' invested in fossil fuels. On an individual basis, though, I have observed that people want this technology in their homes. I for one started my journey towards a comfortable, low-carbon home quite unwittingly, simply because I married a forward-thinking heating engineer.

HOT TIP: THE WAY FORWARD

Don't get tangled up in the politics. Make an independent decision, and you can achieve a real improvement to the comfort of your home.

I want to share a personal triumph. In autumn 2025 my son started his training to become a low-carbon heating technician – a new apprenticeship offered by City College Norwich. I've worked hard to influence the college to offer this course, with one main question fuelling my arguments: *How can we hope to have enough heat pump engineers if we don't have an apprenticeship to train them*? I hope my son will have a long and successful career in heat pump installation.

If *Warm Wisdom* has encouraged you to move forward in your journey to switch to a heat pump, please keep checking for more warm wisdom on the resources page of my company's website: https://rabrown.co.uk/category/resources.

A final point of warm wisdom: go lightly on your journey, doing what you can do to make a difference to the way you live. Be tenacious about making a change without getting hung up on every detail.

Heat pumps are great. I hope you have fun with the transition and many years of warm satisfaction in your newly upgraded, cosy and eco-friendly property.

Industry Deep Dives

This section isn't vital to the process of buying a heat pump, but I am providing additional in-depth material that will be of interest to some readers. If you're interested in the more in-depth industry information, read on.

Microgeneration Certification Scheme (MCS) 2025/26

MCS was created in 2007 by the UK Government, through the Department of Energy and Climate Change (DECC). It was set up to certify installers to deliver solar PV for the Feed-in Tariff incentive scheme, which financially rewarded people for electricity exported to the grid. Its governance altered in

2018 and nowadays behind the service organisation that installers and customers deal with is a charitable foundation, MCS Certified, whose purpose is to give everyone confidence in home-grown energy.[62] The body that installers register with is the MCS Service Company, which is in the midst of a significant redevelopment, with the 'goal... to make every UK home – old or new – carbon free, with energy that's effective, efficient and affordable'.[63]

In their Customer Commitment document, published in January 2025, MCS state that they have 'two main roles – setting and maintaining standards and providing consumer protection'.[64]

What does MCS do that is relevant to you?

MCS assess the quality of registered installers via a number of certification bodies. These organisations check any company's quality assurance records and visit an installation during an annual assessment process. The scheme is in the process of being significantly overhauled in 2025–2026, and MCS are intending to deal with all customer complaints directly from 2026.[65] MCS write and revise the standards your installers work to and stipulate the way some of the information you'll see is presented, eg in the MCS 031.

Is MCS like the Gas Safe Register for the renewables sector?

The aims of MCS and Gas Safe are quite different. A gas engineer's certification and registration are linked primarily to safety. Gas Safe is an individual 'ticket' with a strong legal connotation – because heat pumps have fewer safety issues, personal registration has not been deemed necessary. However, there is potential for poor design and installation of a heat pump system, causing high energy bills and consumer misery.

MCS claim they will be increasing their focus on delivered quality, leading to consistently higher quality installations. They say that their assessment partners will carry out more robust scrutiny of the installations rather than focusing mainly on quality assurance systems, ie the paperwork.[66]

MCS is coming under increasing criticism for failing to deliver on the scheme transition that is now being pushed into 2026.

Things to remember about MCS

Hiring an MCS registered installer should provide you with the following benefits, whichever scheme version they are working to:

- **Access to the BUS grant.** This gives you £7,500 towards the cost of your installation, as long as the installer is also a registered provider for BUS. This information should be shown on an installer's listing on the MCS installer directory.
- **Design standards.** Your installation should be designed in line with criteria detailed in the MIS-3005-D design standard document to ensure your system will adequately heat your house.[67]
- **Pre-sales and contractual information.** MCS dictate how information is presented in the pre-sales (MCS 031) document and also contractual documentation.
- **Customer commitment.** As part of the redevelopment of the scheme in January 2025, a formal document was producing outlining how an MCS registered installer should work with customers.

The installer will:

- Be trustworthy
- Be responsible
- Communicate well
- Contract with clarity
- Carry out a full handover
- Handle complaints well

There is also a list of responsibilities for customers to adhere to.

Monitoring quality and satisfaction

Since the beginning of the BUS scheme, MCS have been contacting all consumers who have received the grant asking for feedback about their installation. This was the beginning of a shift towards a more direct relationship between MCS and both homeowners and installers. This is part of a move from a disjointed situation, where MCS set the standards, while certification bodies (NAPIT, NICEIC, etc) assess the installers against the standards. Historically, these assessments have focused on checking quality assurance systems rather than on assessing technical competence and the quality of the work.

Moving from separate consumer protection

Installers currently need to be registered with both:

1. RECC
2. HIES

These deal with customer complaints and offer a low-cost mediation service if the dispute cannot be quickly resolved. Under the redeveloped scheme, MCS are assuming responsibility for this complaint handling.

Installation standards

MCS also provides a standard for installation (MIS-3005-I). Under the redeveloped scheme, due to be fully introduced in 2026, a named technical supervisor will enter their name into the system, and this will be recorded on the MCS database. This means each installation will be attributable to an individual, which is necessary due to the increase of national installers and umbrella schemes. Certification body assessors need to be able to trace nonconformities to the MCS standards back to the specific installation team who carried out the work.

HOT TIP: MCS HELPLINE

You can call the MCS helpline on 0333 103 8130 with any query about your installer or installation.

The future of MCS

MCS still seem favoured by the government, perhaps due to the original strong ties. There is only one other body competing for their role: Flexible Energy Oversite Registration (Flexi-orb). They have recently received UKAS approval and are hoping to become a viable alternative to MCS.

Other ways to judge the competence and quality of an installer

There are debates in the industry about what other quality assurances might be useful. Three of these are:

1. **Trustmark accreditation.** Some homeowners look for this but with mixed results. I personally feel that Trustmark – the government-endorsed quality scheme – is just another hoop to jump through and doesn't add anything in addition to MCS. It is also of course another cost that needs to be passed on.
2. **Which? accreditation.** This seems to be gaining momentum in the independent part of the sector, and Which? is a well-known brand in consumer quality. I perceive the companies that have added this to their accreditations as high-quality installers.
3. **Octopus Trusted Partner.** Octopus Energy provide a logo with this wording to companies that have passed the Octopus vetting procedure. The process is quite thorough, looking into business health as well as MCS registration, and it is soon to be extended to an Octopus accreditation scheme.

Handy Boiler Upgrade Scheme (BUS) checklist

The BUS is a grant funded by the UK Government that currently pays £7,500 to people installing a heat pump for the first time. It also covers some biomass installations, though to a much more limited degree.

The grant, administered by Ofgem, can be accessed through MCS registered installation companies that are also registered with BUS.

The installer applies for the BUS grant on your behalf. Guidelines for installers advise them to deduct the amount from their payment schedule and show the cost of the heat pump system with the BUS sum deducted on the (quote or) contract that you sign. By signing the contract, you will be agreeing to the condition that if for some reason your BUS application is not successful, you will owe the installation company the deducted £7,500.

Some companies do not follow this guidance as it is not currently mandatory. Instead, they charge the full fee, and after receiving the grant, they refund the £7,500 to the customer. It might seem like a dubious way to operate, and I recommend having a frank discussion with the installation company if they want to operate in this way. It does not mean they are a rogue trader, but speaking from personal experience, I can share that it is very tough to have £7,500 held back on every job. It is particularly difficult with a new-build, where the payment can feel very delayed by the protracted nature of the project. It also feels very precarious for small retrofits, where the £7,500 is a disproportionately high percentage of the total cost.

Private property owners – such as homeowners or private landlords, second-home and holiday-home owners, and private owners of a commercial building – are almost always eligible for the grant. If a domestic property is owned by a company, it is probably not eligible for BUS, although it is always worth checking.

The scheme is split into two types of project: retrofit and self-build.

Process for retrofit applications

1. You need to have an up-to-date EPC for your property before an application can be made.
2. The installation company needs to show on the application the kind of heating system that is being removed.
3. The voucher that is issued when a successful application has been completed is valid for three months. For most retrofit projects the application can be made at the start of the installation.
4. If you are doing building work such as an extension, it is classed as a retrofit project, so you

still need an EPC showing the property at the start of the project before you remove your old heating system.

5. For a new-build project, the installer might wait a little while before making the application. This is because the way the grant works is more geared for retrofit projects. The voucher lasts for three months and then needs to be reapplied for. Over the course of a house build, this can mean several reapplications.

6. Don't worry if the project timings go awry – you can reapply if vouchers expire.

7. The voucher cannot be redeemed until the project is finished and commissioned. The equipment also needs to be registered, and the installation recorded on the MCS database before the BUS voucher can be redeemed; this is when the installer gets paid the £7,500 that they deducted from their quoted price at the beginning of the contract.

8. Ofgem will audit your installation to check it has been carried out as claimed by the installer. This audit may be desk-based or via a site visit.

Process for self-build applications

As your installer effectively administers BUS on your behalf, working with Ofgem, it isn't surprising that they need to pass on the documentation needed to make the application on your behalf. There is more documentation needed for a self-build or conversion project where there was no previous heating system being removed. You need to prove that you are paying for your house to be built. The list below is the documentation we send out, which is deemed by Ofgem to be acceptable evidence:

- Invoices for substantial structural works (eg foundations, timber frame, large order of bricks)
- A letter from HMRC confirming the first owner received DIY house builders VAT refund
- Documentation confirming the receipt of a new-build loan
- Documentation confirming the receipt of a new-build mortgage
- Self-build insurance
- Planning permission

You also need to prove that you own the property personally, ie that it is not owned by a company. Examples of acceptable evidence are as follows:

- Official copy of register of title for England and Wales
- Any legal document to prove who owns the property, such as a solicitor's letter confirming the name of the owner, the address and

description of the land, and the date on which the property ownership was transferred to the grant applicant

Please be mindful of the installer's time in dealing with all this paperwork on your behalf. If you do not provide the information and hence do not receive the grant, your invoice will be £7,500 higher than you are expecting. You will sign a contract agreeing to this, set within the MCS regulated documentation. Self-building is a big project, but it's not fair for your installer to have to keep chasing you for the documentation. If you do not want to apply for the grant, tell your installer, and they can alter your contract to one not including the grant process.

While installers are of course in favour of the grant, the fact that it affects their cashflow is very difficult – having £7,500 outstanding several weeks after the completion of a project is tough. Please therefore be as cooperative as possible in allowing the full completion of the work so that the grant voucher can be redeemed as quickly as possible.

For more details, read Ofgem's 'Guidance for Property Owners'.[68]

Octopus Energy, Heat Geek and other national installers

Octopus Energy entered the installation market in 2022. This coincided with a very challenging time for the heat pump market as the RHI had ended in spring 2022. The economy was at a low ebb, with high energy costs, an economic downturn and high inflation.

Octopus's aggressive advertising campaign was a double-edged sword for established, independent installation companies. It brought the idea of heat pumps to more people's attention, beginning the process of normalising the technology. Octopus's messaging about the types of properties suitable for a heat pump was, however, extremely unhelpful. They had limited heat pump models to offer and hence rejected a large proportion of homeowners making an inquiry. I would describe their model as targeting low-hanging fruit and their pricing as loss leading. One of the Octopus advertising campaigns, offering heat pumps for 'as little as £500', was in July 2025 ruled as misleading.[69]

Autumn 2024: A new direction

In autumn 2024 Octopus altered their strategy. Many companies – including mine – have now been vetted as Octopus Trusted Partners. Octopus listened to feedback from prominent industry figures and realised they had been part of the problem rather than providing the solution, causing an unhelpful disruption in some parts of the market: for larger properties and people undertaking building projects. Ultimately, it is in Octopus's business interest that as many houses as possible switch from gas and oil to heat pumps, as they will then sell more electricity.[70]

The Octopus Trusted Partner scheme

Octopus have changed their script. Instead of rejecting homeowners that express an interest in a heat pump that don't fit the 'vanilla profile':

- They will provide you with details of three locally operating Trusted Partners.
- Octopus are being very careful – they are not giving out customer data to installers or charging companies to be registered as Trusted Partners. They are carrying out a decent level of due diligence vetting of each company and will remove any 'rogue' companies that slip through the net. Octopus are also only partnering with MCS registered firms, and the whole customer journey and contractual arrangement is with the installation company, not connected with Octopus in any way.
- Octopus are hoping that by stimulating the market, manufacturing costs of heat pump units could come down. I'm not sure if this will work,

as the European market for heat pumps is huge and the prices seem to keep going up!

Octopus are currently developing the scheme further and speaking to all Trusted Partners, and I will write an article about this when I know more. You will then find that article on the Resources page of my company's website: https://rabrown.co.uk/category/resources.

Is the future purple?

Octopus offer a range of services in addition to heat pump installation, including solar PV, battery storage and EV chargers. In this way they are covering all bases, with their own directly employed installation teams covering the more straightforward installations, while encouraging other installations by recommending their existing network of quality independent installers.[71] Octopus certainly seem to be innovators, continually updating tariffs and offering new services.

Further information on national installers

Installations are available through other national energy-related companies:

- **Ovo.** Ovo have paired with Heat Geek (see section on Heat Geek below) to install heat pumps.[72]

- **British Gas.** It appears the British Gas model is similar to that of Octopus. They say the installation will take five days, which denotes straightforward retrofit installations.[73]

- **Aira.** Aira use their own installers and are known for delivering heat as a service model but also advertising heat pump installation giving access to the BUS grant. They do not currently have complete nationwide coverage.[74]

- **E.ON.** E.ON offer a range of makes of heat pump and appear to be installing using their own engineers, at least they talk of their own MCS registration.[75]

- **EDF Energy.** Historically, EDF Energy bought an umbrella company, CB Heating, to deliver their installations. Nowadays everything is fully branded as E.ON; they are targeting the retrofit market too and work only on properties with an EPC of D or above. EDF heat pumps have been delivering ECO 4 installations, and there is now a new umbrella scheme for installers to join.[76]

- **Heat Geek.** 2025 has been a year of significant change at Heat Geek. They are offering a new innovative product called ZeroDisrupt, which appears to be aimed at competing head-on with the utility companies' installations. We have just become verified Heat Geeks, as I want to offer this retrofit service under their banner. You will find updates on the Resources page of my company's website: rabrown.co.uk/category/resources.

Some of the reasons homeowners choose to work with Heat Geek directly are because of their:

- Five-year performance guarantee
- Digital platform for all contracts and documents, and for your design materials
- Extended warranties on parts installed
- Ability to switch an installer in the unlikely event anything goes wrong
- Which? trusted trader accreditation
- Real-time monitoring of your system, with tech making sure your installation runs well
- Commitment to providing the very best engineers, which are not only Heat Geek trained but also undergo a further level of vetting and accreditation, including a range of checks on work quality and stability of business[77]

Recommended Further Reading, Podcasts, Videos And Websites

Davis, E and Beanland, B, 'Happy Heat Pump Podcast', www.youtube.com/@happyheatpump-podcast, accessed 29 January 2026

Edgeworth, I, *Welcome to the Wonderful World of Air Source Heat Pumps – What kept you?* (no publisher, no date), available from www.newperspectivels.com, accessed 20 November 2025 – A labour of love, this book is aimed at upcoming heating engineers and dives deep into technical information; great if you want to become a heat pump geek.

Gambling, N, *BetaTalk* podcast, https://betatalk.buzzsprout.com, accessed 20 November 2025 – In-depth conversations with industry professionals. Nathan is an outspoken champion of the heat pump industry, particularly promoting practical skills and training.

Get a Heat Pump, www.getaheatpump.org.uk, accessed 20 November 2025 – Website produced by Nesta and The MCS Foundation

Heat Pump Association (soon to be HPA UK) will be the UK's unified trade body for the heat pump sector, formed by the merger of the Heat Pump Association (HPA), Ground Source Heat Pump Association (GSHPA) and Heat Pump Federation (HPF). Launching in January 2026, it will represent organisations across the full heat pump supply chain, including manufacturers, energy companies, certification bodies, installers, designers, drillers, software providers, and training organisations. For more information see: www.heatpumps.org.uk.

Her Own Space, https://community.herownspace.com/homepage, accessed 20 November 2025 – Retrofit advice forum for female readers, provided by Ellora Coupe (men could try contacting Ellora via LinkedIn). Ellora has also created a forum for professionals called Her Retrofit Space.

Law, J and Litherland, L, *Heat Pumps Unlocked: Real world system design using the 'Heat Geek' method* (no publisher, 2025)

Leary-Joyce, J, *Beginner's Guide to Eco Renovation: Understand the basics and the best questions to ask* (AoEC Press, 2022) – I highly recommend this book, which describes a genuine homeowner journey, sparked by the wish to get a heat pump but without covering that part of the project in detail. It therefore works well as a partner for *Warm Wisdom*.

Mlodzinski, M, *The Ultimate Guide to Heat Pumps: Britain's best installers and experts tell you exactly what to watch for and what to ask* (no publisher, 2025) – Mars has included contributions from over thirty industry experts.

Nesta, www.nesta.org.uk/sustainable-future, accessed 20 November 2025 – A helpful website, their mission being 'to reduce home carbon emissions in the UK by 30% by 2030'

Nesta, 'Visit a Heat Pump Near You', www.visitaheatpump.com

R A Brown Heating Services, 'More "Resources" Articles', https://rabrown.co.uk/category/resources, accessed 20 November 2025 – Warm Wisdom resources on the website of my company. We're based in Norfolk; look me up for installations, inspiration and technical information.

Renewable Heating Hub, https://renewableheatinghub.co.uk/forums, accessed 20 November 2025 – Forum created for homeowners by Mars Mlodzinski

The Happy Heat Pump Podcast, https://thehappyheatpumppodcast.buzzsprout.com, accessed 20 November 2025 – Aimed at homeowners, lovely, informative, straight-talking podcasts. Disturbingly, this podcast was pulled by the BBC even though this was a project Evan was doing independently. Heat pumps are a contentious subject – the oil and gas industry are so powerful they can get BBC employees' side hustles shut down.[78]

Warmur, www.warmur.co.uk, accessed 20 November 2025 – A platform you can use to look at potential running cost savings from technologies and electricity tariffs. This was developed by a tech expert who went on his own retrofit journey. Founder Alex Butcher is working collaboratively, teaming up with former The Heating Hub founders Jo and Caroline. They have also built a home survey tool for installers and are trying to solve the industry skills deficit by creating hybrid training courses. They're creatively tackling many of the pain points of the emerging heat pump industry, and all of this work will benefit homeowners.

Definitions Of Technical Terms And Jargon

Boiler Upgrade Scheme Grant (BUS Grant): The current government-funded incentive, administered by Ofgem, which pays £7,500 to most homeowners and to some owners of holiday homes and private rental and commercial properties. It is an installer-led scheme, with the installer required to apply on the customer's behalf and deduct the value of the grant from their invoices. The installer must be registered with MCS and as a BUS installer.

Borehole: A heat source for a ground source heat pump system. Boreholes, ranging in depth between 75 metres and 150 metres, are drilled by specialist companies and require large rigs. If you want to install a borehole for a domestic system, you will need to check that access is possible. The drilling company will work with the installer to ascertain if the composition of the ground allows for a suitable borehole to meet the calculated heat demand of your property. More than one borehole may be required because they need to be adequately spaced so they do not cool the ground. PV-T is a type of solar panel that can recharge the heat in a borehole.

Buffer vessel: Tanks of varying sizes that store warm water that can be released into the heating system when needed. The purpose of a buffer vessel is to maintain the volume of water available in the system and reduce the number of times the heat pump's compressor needs to turn on and off.

Coefficient of performance (COP): This means the efficiency of the system at any given moment. The calculation an engineer does to provide this figure is to divide the output of heat by the input of energy to produce it. This is usually expressed as a percentage – such as 300% or a number such as 'a COP of 3.5'. The COP figure will be lower on a cold winter day compared with a fairly mild spring or autumn day, with figures ranging from below 300% to above 500% for an air source heat pump.

Compressor: A key component inside the heat pump which moves the refrigerant through the refrigeration cycle while compressing it. Old-fashioned ones were called rotary compressors. More recently there were scroll compressors and a further refinement are inverter-driven heat pumps, which are quieter and more flexible in their output. Stiebel's website says: 'Inverter driven heat pumps speed up and slow down the motor compressor to suit energy demand and use a lot less energy because they follow the needs of the property more closely.'[79]

Cycling (of heat pump): This is the process of the heat pump turning on and off. It is important to remember that the life of the heat pump is linked to the life of the compressor. The more the heat pump short-cycles, the shorter the life of the unit will be, so the ASHP unit should not turn on more than two or three times per hour. Various factors can lead to a heat pump short cycling, including a unit that is oversized for the heat load of the house. Poor controls, where the heat pump is turned on and off with thermostats, can also be detrimental, causing cycling and increased energy consumption.

Distribution network operator (DNO): See 'Electrical Supply Information' in the Resources section on our website: https://rabrown.co.uk/heat-pumps-and-electricity-supply-what-you-need-to-know. There are six DNOs across the UK; in Norfolk we come under UK Power Networks. See the MCS guidance on notifying DNOs: https://mcs-certified.com/notifying-dnos.

Energy performance certificate (EPC): A certificate based on an assessment of your property. In most cases you will need an EPC that is less than ten years old and up to date in terms of insulation, etc, to apply for the BUS grant. One of the figures the heating installer will need from the EPC is the heating and hot water requirement for your property, and many online calculators use this figure to generate a guide estimate. It is important to remember that an EPC's main metric is the cost of fuel to run the house, and that it is biased towards mains gas. A high percentage of EPCs are very inaccurate and determined with no visit made to the property! It is commonly agreed that the EPC is long overdue for reform. It needs to measure carbon emissions rather than focus on fuel prices, which is why it is helpful as only a starting point. A heat loss survey is essential before a heating system design can be produced.

First fix: The initial phase of plumbing and heating work in a significant renovation, conversion, extension or self-build project. Within the first fix, pipes for both plumbing and heating need to be run to the final positions, which might be behind walls and under floors (they won't be attached to anything at this stage). Drainage and sanitary pipes – referred to as 'soil and waste' – need to be laid in this phase too, and pipework needs to be run to the proposed boiler cupboard or plantroom. It is vitally important that all of this first fix work is meticulously planned out with the builder, plumber, heating engineer and electrician, as it is really difficult to alter this later on.

Ground loop: The term for the collector pipe in a GSHP system. Ground loops are flexible pipes that are laid in carefully spaced trenches in clear land surrounding the property, commonly at a depth of approximately 1.2 metres.

Heat curve: A setting, related to weather compensation controls, that adjusts the relationship between the outdoor temperature and the flow temperature of the heating system. The heat curve needs to be adjusted when you begin living with a heat pump system, at the beginning of the first heating season.

Heat emitters: The equipment that the heat pump system is connected to that delivers the heat into the home or building – essentially radiators and UFH. An air-to-air heat pump unit set to heat as well as cool could also be considered a heat emitter.

Heating degree day (HDD): This measures the demand for energy needed to heat a building. It reflects how much the daily outdoor temperature falls below a certain base temperature. Typically, 15.5C is considered a standard indoor temperature below which a building requires heating. The HDD value is a key indicator of heating requirements and energy consumption, providing quantifiable measurements to understand and predict heating needs.

Hysteresis: The term used to describe the temperature set points where a thermostat turns on or off.

On a weather-compensated heat pump system this setting would likely be on your hot water cylinder. The hysteresis setting would typically be 6C, meaning when the hot water temperature had dropped 6C below the set point of say 54C it would switch on to heat up again. The smaller the gap between the on and off settings, the more the heat pump will cycle on and off to top up the temperature. If the hysteresis settings are too large, you could experience an inadequate hot water supply.

Manifold: A component of an UFH system, usually brass or chrome, where the tails of the UFH pipes come out of the floor and are connected, allowing each heating loop to be controlled and balanced. The UFH needs to be balanced at this manifold, and the flow can be adjusted in each zone or loop of pipe. Each zone will relate to a port on the manifold, and a pump will be attached to the manifold. It also has other features such as an air vent to release air from the system. Hot and cold manifolds are a modern way to control plumbing, making it easy to isolate sections of the pipework. These types of manifolds have been used on the continent for a long time and are gradually becoming the norm in the UK too.

Mechanical engineer: Someone who is qualified to design heating and ventilation systems. In larger firms there may be a separate designer or M&E engineer who is not an installer. If the installation company you are looking to use has a designated designer, they are a good person to talk to in-depth about the design.

Microbore pipework: Tiny 8- or 10-millimetre pipes coming up to radiators in many modern houses. These pipes will be teed off from larger pipework (15 mm) behind the wall in the property. It is becoming more common to see retrofit systems in houses with microbore. Sometimes these will be using monitoring equipment such as Adia.

Microgeneration Certification Scheme (MCS): The organisation that sets standards and oversees delivery of installations for heat pumps, solar PV and battery storage.

Monobloc: An ASHP that has the refrigerant gas sealed within the unit – currently the most common type of heat pump. Monoblocs do not need to be installed by engineers with a refrigerant qualification – air conditioning engineers will have the F-Gas (refrigerant) qualification. Conversely, technicians in a specialist air conditioning company may not have the same level of training in designing wet heating systems such as those connected to radiators and UFH.

MVHR: Mechanical ventilation with heat recovery is a whole-house ventilation system that continuously extracts stale, moist air from a house and supplies fresh, filtered air. It works using a heat exchanger to transfer heat from the outgoing air to the incoming air. It saves energy and improves indoor air quality. It's becoming common in modern airtight homes, preventing condensation and mould. It also provides benefits of managing air changes and retains heat while making homes healthier.

Open loop: The principle that the best way to run a heat pump system is with no zoning. If you want to run different rooms at significantly different temperatures, the result can be inefficient in terms of energy usage, with the heat from the warm areas migrating to the cooler areas. The heat emitters then have to work harder in the higher set areas to compensate for the cooler areas.

Permitted development: A term related to planning permission to install an air source heat pump. In most situations planning permission is not required as the air source heat pump can be installed under permitted development rights, but you will need to let the installer know if you live in a conservation area or if your property is listed. Planning permission is also required when installing more than two heat pumps.

Plant room: This term originally referred to the 'boiler room' of a large commercial or industrial building. It is now commonly used in domestic projects and usually means a large cupboard created to house the equipment related to the heating and hot water system. It may also contain manifolds, electrics and controllers. Sometimes an exterior plant room is created in the form of an insulated shed. In many European countries, houses have basements, and plant rooms are located there.

Pumped screed: One of the most thermally efficient coverings for underfloor heating, which sets quickly and transfers heat better than normal cement. You need to inform heating engineers and builders you want pumped screed, then they can arrange the contractor for you. You need the right kind of edging fitted around the UFH so the screed doesn't run into the wrong areas, as it is very liquid.

Retrofit: Judith Leary-Joyce says 'Retrofitting – working your way through the house, putting in new systems that were not in place when the house was built to make it more efficient: solar panels, insulation, new heating systems.'

Seasonal coefficient of performance (SCOP): This is an averaged calculation of the performance and efficiency of a heating system (not just of the heat pump) across a year. MCS standards dictate that the minimum SCOP of a system should be 2.8, or that the system is 280% efficient. Specialist installers aim for significantly better SCOPs; they are not happy with anything less than 3.5 but ideally aim for over 4.

Second fix: The phase of a building project second fix when all the external components are fitted. This includes creation of the plant room and installation of sanitary ware or kitchen.

Thermostat: A traditional on-off control for a heating system. Many houses have been built with thermostats in most rooms, but this is not the best way to control a heat pump system.

Thermostatic radiator valve (TRV): The dial-like knob on the side of the radiator, which can be turned to make the radiator hotter or cooler. In an open-loop system this would be left on full without restricting the heat.

Underfloor heating (UFH): Water-filled heating pipes under the floor, which are most easily installed when a house is being built. There are many solutions for different floor structures.

Volumiser: A tank that stabilises water volume and flow conditions within heat pump systems. Volumisers benefit systems integrating inverter-driven heat pumps, mitigating fluctuations in pump operations, preventing short cycling. Most volumisers are installed on the 'flow side' of the system.

Weather compensation: The way a quality heat pump system is controlled. A sensor in the outdoor unit measures the outdoor temperature, and indoor controls monitor the difference between the outdoor temperature and the indoor temperature. The sensor is ideally sited on a north facing wall to avoid solar gain. When it's cold outside, the controller increases the temperature of the water flowing through your radiators. When it's milder, it automatically turns the temperature down. This benefits efficiency because the lower the flow temperature is, the more efficient the heat pump is at any given time.

Notes

1 Zealux, 'The History of Heat Pump Development: 7 key significant milestones' (Zealux, no date), https://zealux.com/the-history-of-heat-pump-development, accessed 13 November 2025
2 M Zogg, 'History of Heat Pumps – Swiss contributions and international milestones' (Swiss Federal Office of Energy, May 2008), www.ehpa.org/wp-content/uploads/2023/07/History-of-Heat-Pumps-Swiss-Federation.pdf, accessed 13 November 2025
3 Scottish Engineering Hall of Fame, 'Thomas Graeme Nelson Haldane' (Scottish Engineering Hall of Fame, 13 November 2025), https://engineeringhalloffame.org/profile/thomas-graeme-nelson-haldane, accessed 13 November 2025

4 JA Sumner, *Domestic Heat Pumps* (Prism Press, 1975), p9

5 JA Sumner, *Domestic Heat Pumps* (Prism Press, 1975)

6 Ibid

7 P-G Man, 'Building Homes "Not Financially Viable" Across Half of England', *The Telegraph* (26 September 2025), www.telegraph.co.uk/business/2025/09/26/building-homes-not-financially-viable-across-half-of-englan, accessed 13 November 2025

8 B Quinn, 'UK Government Hires "Nudge Unit" to Help Dispel Heat Pump Myths', *The Guardian* (1 January 2025), www.theguardian.com/environment/2025/jan/01/uk-government-dispel-heat-pump-myths-misinformation-media, accessed 13 November 2025

9 *Cooling Post*, 'Historic Country House Places Trust in Heat Pumps', *Cooling Post* (21 January 2024), www.coolingpost.com/features/historic-country-house-places-trust-in-heat-pumps, accessed 13 November 2025

10 C Molloy, 'Ministers Knew Heating Subsidy Was Paying Billions to UK's Wealthiest', *Open Democracy* (10 June 2022), www.opendemocracy.net/en/renewable-heat-incentive-subsidy-conservatives-amber-rudd-ofgem, accessed 13 November 2025

11 UK Parliament Committees, 'RHI Has Failed to Meet Objectives or Provide Value for Money' (GOV.UK, 16 May 2018), https://committees.

parliament.uk/committee/127/public-accounts-committee/news/98454/rhi-has-failed-to-meet-objectives-or-provide-value-for-money, accessed 13 November 2025

12 L Orso and A Sissons, 'One Year In, What Effect Has the Boiler Upgrade Scheme Had?' (Nesta, no date), www.nesta.org.uk/data-visualisation-and-interactive/one-year-in-what-effect-has-the-boiler-upgrade-scheme-had, accessed 13 November 2025

13 J Rosenow, 'Is Heating Homes with Hydrogen All but a Pipe Dream? An evidence review', *Joule*, 6/10 (2022), 2225–2228, https://doi.org/10.1016/j.joule.2022.08.015

14 'Climate Action' (Climate Change Committee, no date), www.theccc.org.uk/climate-action, accessed 14 November 2025

15 HM Government, 'Heat Pump Investment Roadmap – Leading the way to net zero' (HM Government, April 2023), https://assets.publishing.service.gov.uk/media/649d690406179b000c3f751c/heat-pumps-investment-roadmap.pdf, accessed 14 November 2025

16 Dr Jerry Harrall, https://drharrall.com, accessed 14 November 2025

17 N Middleton, 'Huge Concerns About HVO Sustainability Amid Fraud Claims' (Van Fleet World, 11 April 2025), https://vanfleetworld.co.uk/huge-concerns-about-hvo-sustainability-amid-fraud-claims, accessed 14 November 2025

18 'What Is the Most Efficient Heat Pump in the UK?' (Heatable, no date), https://heatable.co.uk/heat-pumps/advice/most-efficient-heat-pump, accessed 14 November 2025

19 B Marks, 'Heat Pump Snippet 3/3: Heat pumps, spark gaps and the invisible hand' (Electrify Research, 18 February 2025), www.electrifyresearch.co.uk/blog/heat-pump-snippet-3/4-heat-pumps-spark-gaps-and-the-invisible-hand, accessed 14 November 2025

20 New Build Inspections, 'Part L Building Regulations & Multi-Zone Heating Systems' (New Build Inspections, 17 January 2025), www.newbuildinspections.com/knowledgebase/part-l-building-regulations-multi-zone-heating-systems, accessed 14 November 2025

21 Nesta, 'Visit a Heat Pump' (Nesta, no date), www.nesta.org.uk/project/visit-a-heat-pump, accessed 14 November 2025

22 J Mullane, 'Leaked Documents Show Gas Boiler Lobby's Attempt to Delay Heat Pump Rollout' (Homebuilding & Renovating, 30 July 2023), www.homebuilding.co.uk/news/leaked-documents-show-gas-boiler-lobbys-attempt-to-delay-heat-pump-rollout, accessed 14 November 2025

23 Channel 5, *Heat Pumps: Are they really worth it?* (TV documentary, Channel 5, 2025), www.channel5.com/show/heat-pumps-are-they-really-worth-it, accessed 14 November 2025

24 Osborne Clark, 'What's Holding Back UK Green Consumer Finance? A Financial Services Perspective' (Osborne Clarke, September 2024), www.osborneclarke.com / insights / whats-holding-back-uk-green-consumer-finance-financial-services-perspective, accessed 22 January 2026

25 J Macmullan, 'Financing for Low Carbon Home Heating' (policy paper) (Which?, September 2025), www.which.co.uk / policy-and-insight / article / financing-for-low-carbon-home-heating-azj8l9O83sXk, accessed 22 November 2025

26 Energy UK, 'Capital Idea to Boost Clean Heat Switch' (Energy UK, 6 August 2025), www.energy-uk.org.uk / news / capital-idea-to-boost-clean-heat-switch, accessed 15 November 2025

27 GoodHeat, 'France's New Regulation on Low-Carbon Heating (2025 Update)' (GoodHeat, 5 July 2025), www.goodheatglobal.com / France-s-New-Regulation-on-Low-Carbon-Heating-2025-Update-id46726006.html, accessed 15 November 2025

28 Department for Energy Security and Net Zero and Martin McCluskey MP, 'Discounts for Families to Keep Warm in Winter and Cool in Summer' (GOV.UK, 18 November 2025), www.gov.uk / government / news / discounts-for-families-to-keep-warm-in-winter-and-cool-in-summer, accessed 5 December 2025

29 HM Revenue & Customs, 'Energy-Saving Materials and Heating Equipment (VAT Notice

708/6)' (GOV.UK, 17 July 2014; last updated 31 January 2024), www.gov.uk/guidance/vat-on-energy-saving-materials-and-heating-equipment-notice-7086, accessed 15 November 2025

30 W Jones, 'How Innovative Finance Products Can Unlock the Market for Heat Pumps' (Elemental London, 17 October 2025), https://elementallondon.show/news/how-innovative-finance-products-can-unlock-the-market-for-heat-pumps, accessed 22 January 2026

31 Heat Geek, 'What Is ZeroDisrupt? The AI that makes heat pumps cheaper than boilers' (14 October 2025), https://youtu.be/shorts/RvURptNDL4k, accessed 22 January 2026

32 MCS, 'MCS2025 – Heat Pump: Design standard' (The MCS Service Company Ltd, 1 January 2025), https://mcscertified.com/wp-content/uploads/2025/02/MIS-3005-D-2025-V1.0.pdf, accessed 16 November 2025

33 H2X, 'Buffer Tanks 101: What they are, how they work, how to size them & do you even need one?' (H2X, no date), www.h2xengineering.com/blogs/buffer-tanks, accessed 18 November 2025

34 Clade, 'Buffer Tanks: Expert insights from a product technical engineer' (Clade, no date), https://clade-es.com/blog/buffer-tanks, accessed 18 November 2025

35 Mars, 'Volumisers in Heat Pump Systems: Does placement matter?' (Renewable Heating Hub,

10 March 2025), https://renewableheatinghub.co.uk/volumisers-in-heat-pump-systems-does-placement-matter, accessed 28 January 2026

36 J Leary-Joyce, *Beginner's Guide to Eco Renovation: Understand the basics and the best questions to ask* (AoEC Press, 2022)

37 Department for Energy Security and Net Zero, 'Warm Homes Plan' (GOV.UK, 21 January 2026), www.gov.uk/government/publications/warm-homes-plan, accessed 31 January 2026

38 dRMM, 'Sliding House – A house for all seasons' (dRMM, no date), https://drmmstudio.com/project/sliding-house, accessed 19 November 2025

39 Nesta, 'Visit a Heat Pump' (Nesta, no date), www.nesta.org.uk/project/visit-a-heat-pump, accessed 19 November 2025

40 Energy Saving Trust, 'Renewables Installer Finder' (Energy Saving Trust, no date), https://installerfinder.energysavingtrust.org.uk, accessed 19 November 2025

41 MCS, https://mcscertified.com, accessed 19 November 2025

42 Heat Geek, www.heatgeek.com/get-a-heat-pump, accessed 15 November 2025

43 Octopus Energy, https://octopus.energy/heat-pump-explore, accessed 15 November 2025

44 www.youtube.com/@RABrownHeatingServices,

45 Nesta, 'Get an Estimated Cost for Installing an Air Source Heat Pump' (no date), https://

products.nesta.org.uk/cost-estimator, accessed 17 November 2025
46 RA Brown Heating Services, 'Heat Pumps and Electricity Supply: What you need to know' (RA Brown.co.uk, 15 January 2026), https://rabrown.co.uk/heat-pumps-and-electricity-supply-what-you-need-to-know, accessed 23 January 2026
47 RA Brown Heating Services, 'Sample Heat Loss Report' (RA Brown.co.uk, 15 January 2026), https://rabrown.co.uk/sample-heat-loss-report, accessed 29 January 2026
48 Mars, 'Is Your 6kW Air Source Heat Pump Really a 6kW?' (Renewable Heating Hub, 8 May 2025), https://renewableheatinghub.co.uk/air-source-heat-pump-output, accessed 29 January 2026
49 Adia, https://adiathermal.co.uk, accessed 18 November 2025
50 Havenwise, www.havenwise.co.uk, accessed 18 November 2025
51 Homely, www.homelyenergy.com, accessed 18 November 2025
52 Open Energy Monitor, 'Heat Pump Monitoring' (no date), https://docs.openenergymonitor.org/applications/heatpump.html, accessed 18 November 2025
53 Hive, www.hivehome.com, accessed 18 November 2025
54 Hive, 'Does Hive Heating Work with my Heat Pump?' (Hive, 23 January 2025),

https://support.hivehome.com/portal/app/portlets/results/viewsolution.jsp?solutionid=250123092600117, accessed 28 January 2026

55 Ofgem, 'Boiler Upgrade Scheme: Guidance for property owners' (Ofgem, no date), www.ofgem.gov.uk/guidance/boiler-upgrade-scheme-guidance-property-owners, accessed 18 November 2025

56 MCS, 'Customer Commitment' (MCS Charitable Foundation, 1 January 2025), https://mcscertified.com/installers/redeveloped-installer-scheme/, https://mcscertified.com/wp-content/uploads/2025/04/MCS-Customer-Commitment-issue-1.0-Jan-2025.pdf, accessed 27 January 2026

57 M Illian, 'What Charles Dickens Can Teach Us About Personal Finance' (Yahoo Finance, 23 July 2013), https://finance.yahoo.com/news/charles-dickens-teach-us-personal-103005122.html, accessed 20 November 2025

58 J Gibbs, 'Hybrid Heat Pumps' (Energy Saving Trust, no date), https://energysavingtrust.org.uk/advice/hybrid-heat-pumps, accessed 31 January 2026

59 N Gambling, 'The Ideal Experience for a Heat Pump Customer', *BetaTalk* (26 March 2024), https://betatalk.buzzsprout.com/509671/episodes/14770059-the-ideal-experience-for-a-heat-pump-customer, accessed 20 November 2025

60 Zehnder, 'General request' (no date), www.zehnder.co.uk/en/contact/general-request, accessed 19 November 2025
61 J Arbib and T Seba, *Stellar: A world beyond limits, and how to get there* (no publisher, 2025)
62 MCS, 'Our role in industry' (The MCS Service Company Ltd, no date), https://mcscertified.com/who-we-are, accessed 20 November 2025
63 MCS, 'Creating a Carbon Free Future' (MCS Service Company Ltd, no date), https://mcsfoundation.org.uk/about, accessed 28 January 2026
64 MCS, 'Redeveloped Installer Scheme' (MCS Service Company Ltd, no date), https://mcscertified.com/installers/redeveloped-installer-scheme, accessed 28 January 2026
65 Ibid
66 Ibid
67 MCS, 'Standards And Tools Library' (MCS Service Company Ltd, no date), https://mcscertified.com/standards-tools-library/?standard_type=new, accessed 28 January 2026
68 Ofgem, 'Boiler Upgrade Scheme: Guidance for property owners' (Ofgem, no date), www.ofgem.gov.uk/guidance/boiler-upgrade-scheme-guidance-property-owners, accessed 18 November 2025
69 J Clarke, 'Octopus Energy advert banned for misleading £500 claim', *Independent* (30 July 2025), www.independent.co.uk/news/

uk/home-news/octopus-energy-ad-heat-pump-b2798563.html, accessed 23 November 2025

70 Octopus Energy, 'Octopus Trusted Partners FAQs' (Octopus Energy, no date), https://octopus.energy/octopus-trusted-partners-faqs, accessed 20 November 2025

71 Octopus Energy, 'Octopus Energy Fires up Heat Pump Rollout with New Installer Partnership Programme' (Octopus Energy, no date), https://octopus.energy/press/Octopus-Energy-heat-pump-installer-programme, accessed 31 January 2026

72 Heat Geek, 'Scaling Impact with Our Partners' (Heat Geek, no date), https://about.heatgeek.com/partners, accessed 20 November 2025

73 British Gas, 'Go Greener for Less with a £7,500 Heat Pump Grant' (British Gas, no date), www.britishgas.co.uk/heating/air-source-heat-pumps.html, accessed 20 November 2025

74 Aira, 'The Aira Heat Pump' (Aira, no date), www.airahome.com/en-gb/heat-pumps, accessed 20 November 2025

75 E.ON, 'Upgrade to Efficient, Low-Carbon Heating with Air Source Heat Pumps' (E.ON, no date), www.eonenergy.com/air-source-heat-pumps.html, accessed 20 November 2025

76 EDF Energy, 'Get an Air Source Heat Pump with EDF', www.edfenergy.com/heating/electric/air-source-heat-pump, accessed 20 November 2025

77 Heat Geek, 'Help Centre', https://go.heatgeek.com/help-centre/the-process#how-we-work, accessed 28 January 2026

78 M Savage and H Horton, '"They dictate the rules": BBC tells PM's Evan Davis to stop hosting heat pump podcast', *The Guardian* (22 April 2025), www.theguardian.com/media/2025/apr/22/bbc-tells-pm-evan-davis-to-stop-hosting-heat-pump-podcast, accessed 28 January 2026

79 Stiebel Eltron, 'Applying Inverter Heat Pump Technology' (Stiebel, 9 July 2013), www.stiebel-eltron.co.uk/en/service/Services-for-partners-and-installers/Email-Newsletter/Email-newsletter-articles/Applying_inverter_heat_pump_technology.html, accessed 28 January 2026

Acknowledgements

When I was younger, I dreamed of being a writer, and I'm delighted now to be sending this book out into the world. I can't say I have enjoyed the many hours in front of the computer, but I'm looking forward to the discussions this book will provoke.

The following people have provided support, encouragement and sanity checking. *Warm Wisdom* would not have emerged in its current form without their help.

First, the person who has been with me the longest on the journey is Scott Keyser, aka The Writing Guy. I feel very fortunate to have had Scott as my writing buddy, and I've done my best to follow his wise counsel to cut out wordiness.

The rest of my beta readers humbled me with their diligence: Dr Amanda Salter (Astra Eco Energy), providing her perspective as a homeowner on the heat pump journey; Anna Saunders (R A Brown Heating Services), my trusted in-house sanity checker; Benoit Siberdt (Nesta), with his broad view of industry knowledge and research; and last but not least, Christine Rigden (Bedworth Church eco-champion), who shared her journey and her enthusiasm.

Special thanks to one of the great collaborators in our industry, Bean Beanland of the Heat Pump Federation, for his support.

Thank you also to those who have shared their case studies – Christine and Terry, Diana and Alun, Laurie and Kathy, and Paul Eastwood.

I've needed the help of R A Brown Heating Services colleagues for technical information, and my thanks go to Richard for talking through how heating systems have worked down the years and sketching diagrams. Also, to Dax Parsons and Simon Youngman for going through our estimating and quotation process in detail, and Amanda Busby for sharing her knowledge of BUS administration.

The Author

Louise Howlett is the co-founder and commercial director of one of the most well-respected heat pump installation businesses in the UK, R A Brown Heating Services. She has been working alongside Richard Brown since 2002, growing the business from two to twenty-five employees. The company has won national awards for their heat pump installation work every year since 2013. Louise was personally awarded Outstanding Achievement of the Year Award in 2024 at the H&V News Awards. This was in recognition of her work in low-carbon apprenticeships and as spokesperson for the industry, setting the record straight on negative press on heat pumps through the Heating Trades Network.

Based in Norfolk, an area of the UK with some of the highest number of detached off-the-gas-grid properties, Louise has the long-term aim of providing a credible alternative to fossil fuel boilers. One of her proudest achievements is the reduction, by thousands of tonnes, in the carbon emissions from the properties where her company has installed heat pumps.

Away from work Louise loves walking the family dog on the glorious Norfolk beaches. She is passionate about wellbeing, a qualified nutritionist and a transformative coach. She aspires one day to have a final career facilitating low-cost retreats, having spent some wonderful weekends working with the Reconnect Retreats team in creating healthy food. Louise likes to make things happen. Her overall ambition, though, is for everyone who wants to install a heat pump at their property to achieve their goal with the minimum of stress and anxiety.

https://rabrown.co.uk

www.facebook.com/rabrownheatingservices

www.linkedin.com/in/louise-howlett

www.linkedin.com/company/r-a-brown-heating-services-ltd

www.instagram.com/rabrownheatingservices

www.ingramcontent.com/pod-product-compliance
Lightning Source LLC
LaVergne TN
LVHW030919080826
845145LV00013B/2970

* 9 7 8 1 7 8 1 3 3 9 7 2 5 *